BATTERED FAITH

A WARRIOR'S JOURNEY FROM DEPRESSION TO DESTINY

CHERYL CHRISTOPHER

Ark House Press
PO Box 1722, Port Orchard, WA 98366 USA
PO Box 1321, Mona Vale NSW 1660 Australia
PO Box 318 334, West Harbour, Auckland 0661 New Zealand
arkhousepress.com

© Cheryl Christopher 2019

Unless otherwise stated, all Scriptures are taken from the New Living Translation (Holy Bible. New Living Translation copyright© 1996, 2004, 2007, 2013 by Tyndale House Foundation. Used by permission of Tyndale House Publishers Inc., Carol Stream, Illinois 60188. All rights reserved.)

Some names and identifying details have been changed to protect the privacy of individuals.

Cataloguing in Publication Data:
Title: Battered Faith
ISBN: 9780648441069
Subjects: Biography; Domestic Violence;
Other Authors/Contributors: Christopher, Cheryl

Cover image courtesy of Alex Perez
Design by initiateagency.com

This book is dedicated to my precious children Jordane and Jerry. You taught me the meaning of unconditional love. I will forever love you my sweethearts.

CONTENTS

Foreword vii

Chapter 1: The Fairy Tale 1
Chapter 2: The End of the Fairy Tale 12
Chapter 3: Reality as She Saw It 22
Chapter 4: Reality's Deception 28
Chapter 5: My Mind versus Me 43
Chapter 6: Faith torn by Depression 60
Chapter 7: Malta - Do I want to be here? 72
Chapter 8: Peaks and Troughs of Faith 85
Chapter 9: There were more 99
Chapter 10: Reality as God Saw It 110
Chapter 11: Jesus understood 128
Chapter 12: Mind vs Mouth 137
Chapter 13: How did I miss the Red Flags? 148
Chapter 14: Abused into Submission 156
Chapter 15: Godly Submission 163
Chapter 16: Gratitude is my choice 176
Final Note from the Author 193

Acknowledgements 203
Bibliography 205

FOREWORD

As a young believer in Christ, I was always pleased to meet fellow Christians at places of work. They allowed me the privilege of meaningful conversations often with a cup of tea. These conversations were a welcome break from the constant hustle at work. I met Cheryl at our work place several years ago; she was smart, efficient and had a great sense of humour. She had the gift to make everyone around her happy and light hearted. After a few conversations, I gathered we had attended the same church at one point. She was married to a successful man who was working for a large organisation; she then had an adorable daughter of whom she spoke of often in the most endearing way. An ideal Christian home, I concluded.

Cheryl had done a masterful job at concealing her true life. This happy go lucky camper was in fact in very trying circumstances. Her mind was riddled with questions both about her life and her Lord. In this book she opens her heart, like she never has before and confides in you as she would with her best friend. She bears her soul and gives you a keyhole view into the dark and disturbing world she endured. You will hear her desperate screams for help and feel the hopelessness of suffering in silence. You will also find the footprints of a warrior charting a course for those weary soldiers who are lost in the world of pain and confusion. You will encounter the mysterious hand of God in her life, working in ways that even leaves her dumbfounded. A love so perfect and unconditional, that it can heal every wound and bring peace to every storm.

The book you hold in your hand probably cost you a few dollars but to the author it has cost her, her whole life and then some more. In its pages you will read the courageous story of a starry eyed young girl who married the man of her dreams only to realise it was no dream but a nightmare.

You will see her struggle, cry, lose her mind and be driven to end her life. You will also see her fight, hold on to the last thread of hope and crawl her way to the light. Her journey is full of disturbing details, desperate prayers and destiny moments.

Buckle up!

Hari Rao
Founder, Get Ready Ministry
www.HariRao.com

CHAPTER 1

THE FAIRY TALE

Lydia was 23 and had finally found the man of her dreams. Richard was everything that she had hoped for and dreamed about for years. He came into her life out of nowhere; she had prayed hard for a *true* Christian and was determined not to settle for anything else. She could almost hear the angels sing 'Hallelujah!' as she stepped into the shop to collect her wedding invites. She was an only child and her parents decided to give her the best wedding possible. She even wrote a poem for the wedding invite that ended with,

'… *You'll forever be mine*', truly believing it.

Lydia spent the next few days thinking about how blessed she now was. She looked back at her life and all the struggles she had overcome since she was sixteen. She had a decent and average upbringing with working parents who had struggled to make ends meet every month. Her daily needs were met by her hardworking parents, but Lydia still felt emotionally empty. She had discovered a lovely church when she was sixteen where she felt accepted. Lydia soon accepted Jesus and was born again. She was so delighted with the decision and she did not regret it one bit, but the pressures of being sixteen were catching up to her.

She grew up in a typical Indian society that took liberty in judging everything with no regard for the individuality of its members. Lydia succumbed to the typical pressures by playing truant and then turned to cigarettes.

Lydia went on to finish her degree where she managed to find a high paying job straight out of university and yet, that seemed insignificant in comparison to her extended family whose children were either engineers or studying towards a medical degree. That was the baseline of a successful education in India, either a doctor or engineer. The call centre industry was booming in India but unfortunately her career choice within that industry was considered average and her society made sure she knew about it. It didn't help her one bit that she was rostered in the night shifts to support the western world's customers, because her society automatically presumed that any woman leaving home at night was headed straight to a brothel.

None of her life choices seem to be the right ones. Nothing she had accomplished was accepted by her society. The pressures were mounting.

Lydia began to feel like a failure. The world was choking her and though she was Christian who was saved, she began to cope with the pressure by turning more to cigarettes and alcohol. She faced enormous societal pressure that if someone was saved, there was no way they should sin… ever, and alcohol and cigarettes were considered sinful in her culture's eyes, especially for a woman. The Indian society did not judge men who smoked or drank, in fact that was considered typical, because a man had to unwind after a hard day.

She was wedged between the judgmental conservative Indian and Christian society and tightly wound family upbringing and did not have the right role model who could teach her to accept herself.

Ever since she started going to a Pentecostal church where the Sunday praise was loud, her life was observed with a magnifying glass by the surrounding society, be it neighbours, family or even her extended family.

Lydia was still extremely passionate about Christianity, but her flaws were glaring in comparison and she began to ask herself, *'How would God be able to look at me, ungodliness and all? How could I serve at church when I was far from being the perfect daughter? How could I lift my hands in worship when those same hands had held cigarettes the night before?'*

The constant struggle of not being good enough for heaven or earth was overwhelming her. She began to pretend to be the model Christian because that's the only way she would be accepted. She had forgotten the essence of being a born again Christian was to be accepted by heaven, but she trying to be accepted by a society that oozed judgement. Soon she was in a catch-22 with herself. *The monster in her head was born.*

Every time Lydia thought she was making progress in her Christian walk, the monster in her head screamed a new label at her, *'Sinner! Failure! Loser! Useless! Liar! Un-talented! Angry! Depressed! Not focussed! Fear! Insecure!'*

She just couldn't run away from it. What was the use of being saved? Didn't the Bible say that once you were saved "… you became a new creation? The old is gone and the new is here." (2 Corinthians 5:17).

She was overwhelmed with shame and guilt and constantly berated herself for falling short of everything she had set for herself. She knew deep down that she needed to step up and stand up for what she thought was right, but that was at the risk of losing friendships and being among the acceptable crowd. *The monster was awake.*

Lydia thought to herself, *'I am never going to get into heaven. I thought that I was a new creation as soon as I was saved. Nothing has changed. No bells. No angels singing hallelujah. No nothing. Everything was the same. The same struggles. The same agony. The same battles.'*

She was caught up in a whirlwind within herself, but she also needed to move on in life.

Lydia soon fell in love with someone but deep down always knew that it could never end in marriage as he was not a Christian and doesn't the Bible say, "… be not yoked with unbelievers… " (2 Corinthians 6:14), but who else would love her as this man did, who had even offered to change his religion for her? Surely he loved her, but something inside kept crying out, '… *this is not your future*' and it grew louder and louder and finally she caved into the voice and ended their relationship. She had to end the relationship to please the ever judging society because she knew the backlash her parents would face if she, a Christian was to marry a man who wasn't. She knew she was making the right decision, an extremely hard decision, and she hoped to the heavens that she would never regret it.

Over the next few months Lydia had faced some of the harshest times, her mind did backflips and began telling her, '*You will never find love again because you aren't that special. You just destroyed the only chance at love. You are not pretty. You are not sexy, and you have nothing that any man would find attractive.*' She was simultaneously pressured by her culture and society to get married because the Indian society automatically resorts to taunting, "What girl doesn't want to get married at 23 and have a child at 24?" Her society automatically, for some reason in their wild group thinking, would begin rumours to get the rest to believe that something was wrong with her. An only child, both parents in good jobs, surely something was wrong with her if she did not want to get married. The rumours would get wild, "Was she having an affair? Was she living a wildly secret promiscuous life? Was she not able to have children? What was a society to think about a girl who refused to get married? Girls got married younger than her, why was she so intent on bringing disgrace to her parents? Was she really a Christian by disobeying her parents?" Her society's twisted pressures clearly mandated, "*A girl must have a good education, not disappoint her family, get married around 22, start spitting out babies and let the man deal with finances and the* job front, while she could stay at home. *She could choose to work, but as long as she didn't earn more than her husband, and she still needed to make sure that she cared for the kids and had food ready on the table because that was a woman's role within the family."* She belonged to a restrictive society and culture and she was now at that terrifying age to fulfil those mandates.

The pressure was mounting as time was now running out. Lydia began to think to herself, '*I do not want to get married. I am working in a great organisation already and I want to set up a career for myself. I know in my society, getting married means the end of my life as I know it.*' She knew that getting married would limit her career and she would have to stop working altogether. She was tired of the minefield in her mind.

Every little thought she had was constantly blown out of proportion. '*If you get married, then you would end up living with your in-laws and having to spit out babies which means, you could not actually go back to work. If you didn't go back to work, your future husband just would not respect you and he would keep you like a servant at home.*' After all, hadn't she seen how her society treated women? They were treated worse than slaves and it didn't really matter if they were employed or not. Just being born a woman alone warranted the treatment they received. In her society's eyes, women did not deserve anything close to the male privilege.

Hadn't she seen her mother, an extremely intelligent, employed woman constantly fighting to not be treated like a slave by men, some who were neither intelligent nor employed? '*Was I destined to become like one of these women who end up a statistic? Was I going to end up on the list of women who were burned to death by their in-laws for a dowry? How many children I was expected to birth? Oh Lord… what if I couldn't have children? That would be the ultimate humiliation… not being able to have children.*' These thoughts began to eat her, but all the while Lydia learned to walk around with an iron clad mask that hid the pain and torment. She started wondering if suicide was the answer to her fear and anxiety. She was barely able to function on a daily basis without irrational fear of her future creeping in. *The monster was awake and had begun its work.*

It was all she could do to ignore her own emotional state of having broken up with a man she loved so she could marry an unknown Christian man to raise an acceptable Christian family. Surely the least she could do was satisfy society into thinking that nothing was wrong with her and save her family from humiliation by proving that she wanted to get married. She finally decided to sacrifice her emotions and ignore every feeling of insecurity she had, and told her mother that she was ready for them to find a man for her. She desperately hoped that she would not regret this decision.

The family set about finding what her culture labelled as the 'eligible bachelor'. She took an empty book and called it 'Prince Charming' and began to write in it what marriage meant to her, praying while writing every sentence. Her list began to grow as she included in it everything she wanted in a marriage. Lydia did not just want a wedding, she wanted a marriage and wanted, more than words could describe, a man who would go to sleep praising God and wake up praising God and teaching their future children about the gracious God she knew and loved. She battled between knowing that she had to pray about this decision and also fighting the fact that maybe God was never actually going to listen to her because of her glaring imperfections.

People recommended using matrimonial websites that were safe and so they did. The first 'eligible bachelor' came along and was a doctor who really liked her and promised to give her the world. At 22, her shallow mind thought, '... *oh dear! He's much older than me, plus he's bald! How can I live with a man who looks older than my grandfather?*' She told her mother that she could not marry him, hoping that she would not regret this decision. A few others came along, but all she could think about was 'Prince

Charming' and how none of them would fit her list. Her mind, a miserable negative chatterbox, began to play tricks by telling her, '… *your list is your way of sabotaging your future. You're never going to meet a man who will fit your list. You don't want to get married and you're hiding behind your book.*'

The matrimonial agency would do extensive searches and checks and would regularly post copies of all 'eligible bachelors' to her home and she'd flick through them and throw them out, until one day… one day when she saw the perfect man. He had beautiful brown eyes and the most gorgeous smile she had ever seen. He looked like he had the softest deep brown hair and carnality made her long to run her fingers through his hair. Everything about him was perfect and so natural. Even his name, Richard, sounded so perfect and elegant. It was his name that first drew her attention; he didn't have an Indian name. It seemed like a petty thing, but it meant a lot to her.

How she admired him. Lydia knew straight away that he was the one if there was such a thing. She believed in soulmates and she desperately wanted to believe he was hers. She told her mother Anne, who promptly called his parents. "They sounded nice," her mother said. "He's got a great job and his parents are pastors and have five churches in the outskirts of a large metropolitan city."

Anne, who was a well-educated and astute woman, asked Richard's mother, Esther what his qualifications were, as education was one of the highest priorities of her culture and society in finding a prospective mate. Esther simply said, "Richard had studied a lot, but only he knows his actual qualifications. You'll have to ask Richard yourself." How strange, was that a red flag that his parents had no idea what their only son had studied? '*Of course not,*' Lydia thought aloud. '*Maybe he had worked and studied while he lived in the different cities of the country, and that probably explained why his parents had no idea about his qualifications.*'

After Anne spoke to Richard and gave Lydia the approval that he decidedly was a nice young man, Lydia then began her relationship with him, getting to know him. She spoke to him for hours every night for a whole week, and one night as she was leaving work, Richard said, "I have something to tell you. I love you." Lydia was speechless. She had only known the man for eight days, and they had a relationship that was only over the phone. She had never even seen him face to face. Her shallow windbag mind screamed, *'Do you even know if he has both legs or is mentally stable?'* She simply said, "I'll speak to you later" and hung up the phone and tried to calm her nerves.

Lydia's parents decided to go to his home city and meet with his parents and then a few weeks later he would come with his parents to her home, all part of her intricate and elaborate cultural requirements of an 'arranged marriage'. She now began to feel butterflies in her stomach. Her monster was back to its old tricks again, *'What if his parents say no to you? You are not that special.'* She genuinely was terrified when Richard told her, "If my father, a self-proclaimed prophet, said no to our relationship, then I have to obey my father's wishes." Was that her next cause of concern? But, how was she to know, her mind's voice was louder than any rational thinking. So, Lydia waited. Richard called her later that day after both their parents had met and said, "God had told my father that this union was approved by God." She thought to herself, *'I'm a Christian too. How come I didn't hear God say anything? Maybe it's because I am not always praying and not running churches or fasting all the time. I really am not that special.'*

Lydia didn't let these thoughts bother her for more than a few minutes, she was ecstatic. After all the emotional and societal struggles since her teenage years, finding true love was her greatest priority. She was going to marry Richard. She was going to be loved forever. She waited for the day when she finally would see him in person for the first time after all those weeks of a phone relationship. Dressed in her finest traditional wear she waited to see him. She loved him the minute he stepped out of the car.

She looked at him and realised she had built a deep bond over the few weeks of phone conversations. As the families continued their conversations, just before lunch Richard looked at Lydia and said, "Can you show me where I can wash up?" Lydia happily led him and suddenly he grabbed her and kissed her. The thrill of it, with the parents in the next room drove her mad. Such behaviour was unheard of in her culture. Everyone there was absolutely prim and proper. She knew then that her marriage would be perfect. At dinner, she felt an emotional connection with him and knew that this marriage would last forever.

Richard even bought her a necklace the next day. She treasured it and wore it everywhere. Traditional engagements in her culture happened with great pomp and ceremony, and hers was no different. The odd thing about it was only three people from his family showed up and it was a little unsettling, but Lydia put it down to the expenses of travelling to another city. The engagement was also the time where the families would discuss the financial planning as a half-half split for the wedding itself. Her parents wanted her to have the best, and Richard's father Joshua said, "The bride's family has to bear all the expenses and the groom's side will bear nothing." This red flag she acted upon immediately and told Richard, "The wedding is off as my parents would in no way bear the entire expenses for the wedding with over three thousand guests." Reluctantly, after some discussion, they came to an agreement to bear *some of the expenses* and she was grudgingly satisfied.

Lydia put the incident behind her and began to prepare her mind for her wedding and their lives together. Richard lived in a different city and asked her to come over to the new apartment he had moved into so she could see for herself the place he had set up for her. Six weeks before her wedding, she went over with her family and she loved the effort he had put into making the home look lovely. She fell in love with him all over again. That night, as her family slept, she sat on the couch watching television with him. They spoke about their future together and she felt extremely comfortable with him. She fell asleep and suddenly she was woken up when she felt him lying on top of her kissing her. She panicked and pushed him away. She said, "No! Just a few more weeks and we'd be married, let's not do anything now." She couldn't make any noise to wake her family as that would probably mean they would call the marriage off but she loved him and didn't want that to happen. She battled the decision alone in the heat of the moment and she tried really hard to fight Richard off... unsuccessfully.

She sat up in utter shock, humiliated, ashamed and scared. She couldn't look him in the eye as he said, "you were great." The humiliation of being objectified by the supposed man of her dreams began to slowly cripple her. She ran into the bathroom, bleeding and terrified and burst into tears, sobbing uncontrollably as her mind flooded with echoes of, *'Was I just raped? Does it count as rape? Does it mean rape if it was a man I think I love? I'm sure I love him... do I? He doesn't seem to be bothered by it... should I be concerned about that? He's going to be a pastor and is the son of a supposed pastor... surely he believes that premarital sex is not ok. He's trying to convince me that I did consent... so maybe I did... but I didn't, did I? Maybe I sent him the wrong signals when I decided to fall asleep on the couch. I really should've been more careful. I should have been clearer when I said no... because the man I love or who says he loves me would never force himself if I was clear or assertive enough. I've messed up again! What if I get pregnant now? Oh God, now that's just going to destroy my family. How will they face the social stigma? It's all my fault. I just can't get anything right.'*

She had no idea how long it was before she decided to come out of the bathroom and he wasn't there. Richard was in the lounge watching TV. She stood in the hallway and looked at him and was horrified at how insensitive he was, but she convinced herself that he probably waited and went back to the lounge because she was in there for too long.

Lydia looked into his eyes seeking some comfort, some reassurance… some anything. He just smiled at her like nothing happened. Her intellect immediately made excuses for him. *'He's probably not good at expressing himself. He's not going to understand what you feel like if you don't tell him.'* So she did. He simply said, "Call my mother and tell her I raped you." It was like he had brought a sledgehammer crashing on her face. Her mind screamed, *'Get out of this relationship now. Call the wedding off. He's asking you to cry rape so he can deny it. He should be calling his mother, not you. It was rape. You were raped!'*

Lydia was six weeks away from marrying a rapist.

CHAPTER 2

THE END OF THE FAIRY TALE

Lydia entered the marriage with the dark secret shame looming over her. Would it ever be the same? It was a secret that she held close and was ashamed to tell anyone. She hoped that marriage would somehow erase that shame as she justified it to herself, *'It must be ok because I married the same man that forced me into sex before marriage…it must be ok.'*

The wedding was absolutely lovely and she enjoyed the grand pomp and celebration that went along with an Indian wedding. That night after the exhaustion and the reception that went past midnight, she took off her heels and slumped on the couch excited by the many wedding gifts. She started to open them up one by one, and watched Richard sulk in the corner. She asked, "What's wrong?" He looked at her, angry but tried to hide it, "You've been opening gifts for over half an hour now. It's our first night, the wife is supposed to sleep with her husband." Lydia was shocked and appalled, but she figured that this was how marriage worked. She had seen it on TV, the Indian silver screen had always glorified the *first night* after marriage between a man and his wife as purely raw and sexual. She accepted this as the norm and didn't want to offend her new husband. She accepted that giving in to Richard's every wish was now her life, because that was the role of a woman.

Lydia tried her best to keep the peace in their marriage. She watched Richard sulk every time she was on the phone with her friends, so she slowly stopped her conversations with her friends. Every time she spoke to her mother over the phone, Richard would say, "Everyone is more important than me to you." She was torn between her own emotional needs and satisfying her husband. She chose the latter because she believed that he was her future and she needed to keep him happy at all costs.

Their first real fight was a few months into their marriage, where she discovered Richard had taken a significant bank loan without telling her. She asked him, "Why didn't you tell me?" He answered, "My father had prophesied that I was to take the loan but not tell anyone." Right away, she knew this was wrong. She chose to ignore it but was extremely vigilant, or so she thought. She was living with him in a different city and she had never felt more helpless. She couldn't tell her parents every single thing that was going wrong because they would be utterly destroyed, so she battled with it alone. Lydia's mother Anne would call and speak to her every night and although she sensed something was wrong in her daughter's life, she didn't think it was anything serious. It seemed like the usual struggles and hiccups of a new marriage.

Lydia slowly watched Richard's bank statements stop coming home and he told her that they were now online, but she never got a glimpse of them. A few months later when Lydia visited her in-laws, Esther seemed to have all the copies of the same bank statements that had supposedly gone online.

Lydia was fuming, but she decided to hold her peace for the sake of her marriage. It was just bank statements after all.

Richard deviated her focus from the bank statements and he told her stories of how only his parents were allowed to prophesy to their five churches, and how God supposedly spoke only through his mother Esther. Richard told her that Esther would tell the members of the church that everything going wrong in their lives was only because of adulterous sin. Though Lydia struggled to cope with these ridiculous unbiblical concepts and she was sure that Richard's parents were destroying the emotional state of the people around, she still tried to help with their church, because she thought that she was a part of the family. However she was firmly kept in the dark and simply could not understand why her husband refused to let her get involved in their churches. She offered to help set up a children's ministry for them, using her experience with the ministry in her own church, but she was met with a response that simply was, "God never told us to do such things!" With ear-splitting alarm bells ringing, she decided that this was not her destiny to follow.

Frustrated, she finally gave up on doing anything with their churches and decided instead to focus on her family but she definitely wanted to get involved with the budget and the running of the family.

She did not expect to hit a stone wall again, where Richard continued to refuse to show his bank statements or have her involved. Lydia called Esther, expecting her to speak some sense to him, but another shock rocked her when Esther said, "You have no rights over what he earns or what he does with his money. You just need to be grateful for what you are getting. Be grateful that at least you have food on the table every day. " She was shocked as she hung up the phone and couldn't do anything about it.

Richard told Lydia that he was paying his tithes, or one-tenth of his salary, into his family's church but Esther stubbornly said that they had not received any money from him. Lydia tried to reason with Richard's parents about his lies and how frustrated she was but Esther took it one step further, "Stop complaining about my son. Be grateful that I'm a Christian lady because you have no idea what I'm capable of doing to you!"

At that point, eight months into their marriage and pregnant with their first child all her love for Richard began to drain as Lydia saw the fairy tale illusion fade.

She discovered that she had more peace at work but strangely, Richard would force her to show him all her bank statements and would question her about everything she spent.

Her first mistake, she realised a little too late, was being completely truthful to him about her past. She had told him about her past failed relationship and he had seemed genuinely concerned and supportive. She soon realised that those were just words. Richard began to doubt her whereabouts when she wasn't in his line of sight. He constantly called her asking her where she was and what she was doing and whom she was with. It got worse when she was forced to work night shifts to continue to build her career. Lydia had to leave for work at the same time Richard returned home from his job.

He hounded her to explain every single thing she did, including why she needed to work and why she needed to work nights, refusing to believe that she was rostered on nights. He would wait outside her work place late at night to make sure that she was really at work.

Lydia dealt with his growing paranoia on a daily basis where he thought that she was having affairs all around the town when she was at work. Life was getting increasingly frustrating when he turned up to work night after night to check up on her.

Lydia began to see Richard for who he really was, paranoid and apathetic in every sense. One instance when she was pregnant and had been to visit her in-laws, she faced utter humiliation when her father-in-law walked into her room unannounced and said, "Change your dress, your chest looks ugly in that dress. Your top is too tight." She was speechless and stunned, but she lived in a culture where no one ever spoke back to an elder. So she told Richard about how humiliated she felt, but he simply said, "It's no big deal. Stop making a big issue about everything. You hate my family and that's why you want to nit-pick at every little thing."

Lydia's anger and hatred towards him began to grow, but she felt that she had to love him because her fear of ending up alone made her let every humiliation slide.

Richard had slowly conditioned her to ignore all the warning signs. He had started controlling everything she did and he was masterful at doing it so subtly that she didn't even realise it was happening. He even refused to let her drive and said, "You need more experience. You might crash. You aren't an experienced driver like me. It's better that I drive." She did not realise that he had discovered her anxiety and knew that his words would cause her more anxiety and she began to tell herself and others, "I prefer not to drive. It is better Richard drives because he's a better driver." Something that seemed so insignificant at the time was a massive sign that she missed because she believed that he was looking out for her, but Richard knew that he was slowly stripping her of her self confidence and he couldn't believe how simple it was. '*Stupid Lydia,*' he thought to himself, *do you really think that you're smarter than me? Let the world see that women really are the weaker sex.*'

Lydia didn't see the maliciousness when he had said, "You're going to be a lousy mother" when she was three months pregnant because she was feeling too sick to serve him dinner. She didn't realise it was sexual abuse when he forced himself upon her almost every night. He minimised everything he did to her and she began to accept this as part of the marriage. She did not know any different and spousal abuse was a topic everyone avoided - because her culture believed that it did not count as abuse if it was within a marriage. No one spoke about it. Fewer people even considered spousal abuse a real thing. She didn't know any different and so, Lydia ignored his stubbornness in refusing to show her his bank statements. She ignored Richard's hurtful words of calling her a whore. The more she ignored the signs, the faster he conditioned her mind to erase the signs. She could not see his apathy when she was so angry with his dishonesty and he manipulated her and twisted it around to make her blame herself for ruining their evening. She did not see him push her to self-harm because he now could shift the blame on her and had a new route to blame her and label her insane. She slowly accepted it as the norm when Richard began to doubt her whereabouts at work and every minute that she was out of his sight. She didn't worry too much when she caught him on several occasions watching pornography because she figured *men have needs*. She was completely blinded to him fuelling his vices with all the money he could get his hands on. She was conditioned to ignore her father-in-law who told her that it was a disgrace that she had given birth to a girl as her first child and when her husband laughed at it. She began to submit to the lowly state of a slave. She continued to stay quiet when Richard would snub her rudely if she as much asked who he was on the phone with and he would say, "It's none of your business."

She didn't understand but accepted it when he refused to let her spend any time at after work events. She accepted that it was best for her to avoid all work events because that just led to nasty fights at home.

Lydia was now used to Richard's jealous angst. His sly nature had now moulded into her marriage and Lydia resigned to what it was. While others saw him as the sweet spouse holding the door open for her, only she felt him subtly push her through the door. She began to get used to the fake smile Richard gave her after. She accepted it when he began forcing her to have another child because his father had prophesied that they would have three children. She saw him send money to unknown overseas accounts but she couldn't do anything about it. She preferred to play the mute than to go through the rigmarole of the verbal and psychological abuse that lasted days. At the beginning of the marriage Lydia initially refused to be the first one to apologise, but she was getting exhausted with her marriage and each argument that lasted for weeks and ended only if she apologised. She soon figured that her apologising was the only way to get some peace back into her life, but she had another problem to deal with.

Richard now began to hold her apology as a trump card and said, "Why would you apologise if it wasn't your mistake? You're clearly the problem in the family." She just couldn't win.

She slowly began to withdraw into a shell and avoided any conversation that might be the slightest trigger. She was walking on eggshells in her marriage. She said nothing when she had to mow the lawn while being eight months pregnant with her second child, while Richard watched a movie in the lounge. She had become de-sensitised to his narcissism and his attitude that some chores were beneath him. She played dumb while she watched him text someone on the phone the whole night while she was in the labour room giving birth. She resigned to her fate when she began to dislocate her shoulder on numerous situations because her body was getting weak and she no longer could carry her new born boy safely after bathing him. She asked Richard for help but accepted his rudeness when he said, "It's not my problem. You're the lady and the child is your job."

With the baby just a few weeks old, Richard began to hound her appearance, "Maybe you shouldn't wear that dress. You've gained so much weight. You need to start taking an effort to look better." Lydia's self worth and self esteem began to wane. She started hating herself and everything about her appearance.

She continued to watch him squander away the money but was still unable to say anything. She silently watched him fuel his vices with the money he said he was paying to the church and she began to wonder if anyone was ever going to stop him. She watched him rake up so much debt that it was now crippling. Every time she brought up the question of the rising debt, Richard snapped, "It's all for you. You're the one wasting all the money." She just didn't understand because it had been several months since she had bought anything for herself and with a baby less than six months old, she began to struggle with her mental state.

She heard him spread rumours to his family over the phone when he said, "I am certain that the kids are not mine. I think Lydia is sleeping around." She just could not understand why her life was beginning to spiral out of control. Why was Richard doing this to her? She was struggling with her marriage on a daily basis and she began to detest his lies and Richard's perfect ability to twist everything to suit his schemes. She began to realise that he only wanted for her to be drained in every imaginable way, physically, emotionally and financially. That was the only way that he could continue to assert his control over her.

She was frustrated with his lies and she sensed that there was more to who he was. Lydia knew there was a greater secret that he was hiding from her. At her wit's end, she went to bed that night still unsettled. She looked at Richard fast asleep and her heart just didn't sit right. She was so disturbed.

She fell asleep almost immediately and suddenly, she felt a hand on the back of her neck. She was terrified and her whole body froze and yet she couldn't scream. The hand dragged her to the guest bedroom and pushed her on the bed. Lydia could not move her body as she lay frozen on the bed weeping uncontrollably. She was certain that Richard had dragged her to the other room and now he was going to kill her, and she lay on the bed waiting for his murderous rage to begin. Suddenly, she heard a man in a hushed whisper, "You will see his true colours" and in her mind's eye Lydia could see her living room and a thick dark cloud descending on her husband. Everything fell deathly quiet just as quickly as it had begun.

The words, *'Praise His name'* repeatedly bellowed through her brain over and over until she began to shake in her bed and the words broke into a song that she had never heard before. She was not sure what time she fell asleep and woke up only when Richard came into the guest bedroom and asked her, "Why did you spend the night in a separate room?"

She softly replied, "I had a severe headache and needed to just be alone." She didn't go to church that morning with the rest of her family because her body still ached. She sat on the edge of the bed and thought about her horrendous dream last night. She couldn't understand the horrible dream. She shuddered as she thought of the man's hand on the back of her neck. She had a horrible pain in the same spot and she assumed that when someone has an intense dream their bodies react as well.

She stood up in tremendous pain to walk to the bathroom. She stood in front of the mirror and rubbed the sides of her neck. Lydia's body froze in absolute horror. She stared at the mirror, her eyes motionless. Her throat went dry and she felt faint. She could see a purplish-blue bruising. She was confused and suddenly was not sure if this was a bad dream too. She picked up another mirror and held it awkwardly trying to see the back of her neck. She craned and strained and she gasped in horror as she saw the huge bruise covering most of the back of her neck.

Instinctively, she looked towards heaven and screamed out in anger, "Why are You doing this? What am I to You? Leave me alone." She just couldn't understand what was going on. She didn't feel like any of this was real. She was certain that she was now demon possessed. She just could not fathom what was happening or why. Lydia still stood shaking in terror in front of the mirror, and although she was alone, a song began playing around her *'when everything falls apart, praise His name.'* She had never heard the song but something familiar about it slowly began to comfort her. She was convinced she was going insane. She was convinced she had finally lost her mind. She was stunned at the plethora of emotions her mind had just been subjected to and yet she wasn't sure what to make of it.

Lydia finally managed to calm down and recuperate after the ordeal. She went to Richard the next day and said, "I had a dream about a dark cloud coming down on you…" and the words had hardly left her mouth when she shuddered at the murderous look in his eyes. Lydia saw something in Richard's eyes that she had never seen before and she was terrified. She immediately decided to continue sleeping in the guest bedroom.

The next day her bank called her about the rising debts in their account and she was furious. She confronted Richard again about his bank statements as they were slowly sinking into a rising debt. He told her, "If you want answers, speak to my mother." She was taken aback, but finally reaching breaking point, she called Esther, still angered by the fact that she had to speak to someone who really had no business being involved in their financial situation when she herself was kept in the dark by him. Lydia will never know what made her choose to record the whole conversation but she watched Richard's hackles go up.

CHAPTER 3

REALITY AS SHE SAW IT

Evil comes from the abuse of free will.
~C.S. Lewis

That night, Lydia knew she had let a lot slide. She heard her mother-in-law Esther tell her over the phone, "You whoremonger! How dare you ask my son for an account of his money? What right do you have?" Lydia was shaking with a myriad of emotions and was overcome with shock as she saw Richard grimacing and fear rolled over her as she called out to her mother, "Ma, record this now." Anne, terrified of the situation hurriedly came carrying the phone to record the situation that was very quickly escalating. That moment, something within Richard snapped. He was holding their five-month baby and his 'true colours' made him throw the baby into his crib and come after Lydia to strangle her.

He had just heard his mother shame Lydia and he was furious that he was unable to savour that victory because he had expected Lydia to cower in shame but she was fighting back. He couldn't imagine Lydia now trying to gain control of her life. How dare she try to fight back! He knew he had to put an end to this and he lunged at Anne and attacked her. Lydia watched their little seven year old daughter Joy scream in horror as the violence and abuse unfolded before her young eyes.

Joy watched her father assault her mother as the chairs flew across the lounge. In the midst of the children's screams of fear and absolute horror and the yelling, in the midst of the scratches on her body, Lydia did the unthinkable. Little Joy was still screaming as her face was pale with terror, "Stop it! Stop fighting! Why are you fighting? Stop it, papa."

Lydia called the police. She called the police on the man who promised nine years ago at the altar that he would protect her. Lydia called the police knowing her society would shame her and she would be denigrated for the rest of her life. She was shaking as she gave the details of the abuse over the phone. She saw Richard glowering at her, and just as quickly as he had lunged at her, he sat on the couch and the police walking in five minutes after the phone call were met with a scene of absolute calm on his face.

The anger, the shaking, the tears, nor the children's screams seemed to have any impact on Richard as he smiled at the police, almost like he was welcoming them home to dinner.

The police read the messages Lydia had sent to Anne that said she was scared for her life, but Richard kept repeating, "I was set up. I was set up to attack. She wants me to get into trouble." He suddenly realised that this version did not add up, so he immediately said, "I never intended to attack. I actually never hit her or her mother. She's just creating drama. Lydia always wants attention and her intention has always been to trap me." The police heard everything they needed to and finally, they issued Richard with an order to leave the property for two days. He left the house, but not before making a snide comment, "I have to leave the house that I am paying for and you are still staying here!" Lydia watched her husband walk out the door escorted by the police officers and part of her was broken, but a part of her could not comprehend what had just unfolded. She was infuriated by his sense of smugness and she was suddenly in a situation that was more than she bargained for. In that moment, she knew that her marriage was over. She went to her room and knelt on the floor and cried. She wept until her eyes were sore as Joy hugged her and said, "I'm here for you mummy."

She didn't know how long she walked around her lounge before she suddenly picked up the phone and decided to speak to some members of Richard's family whom he had refused to let her speak with previously. Very quickly, she knew why. Lydia understood Richard better after that two-hour conversation with his extended family than she had in the last nine years.

She was unsettled when she found out that nearly fifty years ago, her in-laws, both from different religions had fallen in love and got married, despite their own families not being supportive of it. It just did not make any sense. It was unheard of to fall in love and marry someone without the family support, especially in the Indian society in the early seventies. They belonged to a country and culture where falling in love was unheard of and some families had been shamed and humiliated even to the extent of being forced to take their own lives. There have been public beatings that sometimes led to murders if the so called 'moral police' saw a girl and boy as much as speaking to each other. Lydia was convinced that her in-laws had not fallen in love, especially not in such a conservative society or country as hers. If they had married without their family support, then they would have had to hide away and live in shame, but this was opposite to the life that they were living.

She sat quietly and listened to uncover that her father-in-law, Joshua came from extreme poverty but now had complete control of his wife's money and properties. Joshua had quickly discovered Esther's family who ran a few churches and were possibly going to hand their estate over along with the finances to one of their daughters and he had to get the money into his power to make a status for himself.

Lydia began to reflect on her own situation and piece together what she thought was a possibility. Joshua had probably forced himself on Esther, exactly like Richard had on her, and maybe had gone on to blackmail Esther and her parents. *History had repeated in her life.*

Esther had to live through the brunt of that shame and was forced to marry him. Lydia now understood why Joshua had all the financial control of the churches and properties that actually belonged to Esther's family. She understood why Esther believed so strongly that it's best for the woman to stay out of the man's business - whatever that might be.

Then suddenly the smoke and mirrors cleared away and she understood the family that she had married into. She understood the love of money they had and the insatiable greed for mammon. A voice began repeating in her head *what you tolerate, you cannot change.* Lydia began to understand her husband now. She understood the impact of Richard's learned behaviour from his father and she saw the desperate need to control women. She saw the horrible controlling power that her husband was oppressed by all his life. *What you tolerate, you cannot change.* She saw the real puppet master - her father-in-law Joshua. He was the controlling force behind it all and was the master manipulator. She suddenly saw the gravity of the little things, like why Richard refused to enter a cinema to watch a movie, even if their daughter Joy wanted to, because Joshua had declared that going to the cinemas was immoral. Richard lived in fear of Joshua and could not stand up to him, so he chose to watch movies and porn on his laptop keeping it out of the public eye. Joshua would never know what Richard did on the sly. That was all that Richard was worried about. He needed to submit to the alpha male in the pack. *What you tolerate, you cannot change.*

Lydia suddenly understood all the years of his double standards. She pieced together Richard's need for power that he displayed. *What you tolerate, you cannot change.* She realised that he would never be free to live his own life, until he could see the obvious and break away from the clutches of his controlling father. She understood that his father had emotionally blackmailed him into thinking that God would curse him if he ever stood up to his parents - no matter how unscrupulous. *What you tolerate, you cannot change.* She understood why money was so important to his father and why, as a pastor, Joshua had once told her that giving to God was not a law according to the Bible, and yet on Sundays, he would force his church members to give him money. Money gave him power to control. *What you tolerate, you cannot change.* She saw the family who deceived people by saying they hear from God in every instance of every second of every day, including the absurdity of which restaurant God led them to dine at. Joshua had discovered an easy money making route and Esther just had to submit, whether she agreed or not. It didn't take long for her to realise the pleasures that money could buy so she joined forces with Joshua too. They could now have it all, money and status.

Lydia realised that these self-proclaimed God-men were nothing more than liars who had discovered the easiest money making avenue amongst the gullible-and she was one of them. *What you tolerate, you cannot change.* She had believed that she was intelligent and would be able to see right through any lies and deception. She felt the carpet pulled from under her feet and Lydia felt herself falling on her face as the reality of her intellectual capacity set it. *What you tolerate, you cannot change.* She had just wasted nearly ten years of her life being deceived by a man who had the aura of an angel. No one but her saw the horns beneath the halo. She was stunned into silence as she realised that she had a decision to make, a life-changing decision.

"God created things which had free will. That means creatures which can go wrong or right. Some people think they can imagine a creature which was free but had no possibility of going wrong, but I can't. If a thing is free to be good it's also free to be bad. And free will is what has made evil possible. Why, then, did God give them free will? Because free will, though it makes evil possible, is also the only thing that makes possible any love or goodness or joy worth having. A world of automata - of creatures that worked like machines- would hardly be worth creating. The happiness which God designs for His higher creatures is the happiness of being freely, voluntarily united to Him and to each other in an ecstasy of love and delight compared with which the most rapturous love between a man and a woman on this earth is mere milk and water. And for that they've got to be free."
~C.S. Lewis

CHAPTER 4

REALITY'S DECEPTION

Lydia had not spoken to anyone about the pain and loss of her marriage. She had not yet grieved for the loss of ten years of her life and her dreams. She had still not totally managed to wrap her head around why this had happened to her. Her mind darted between if she was the reason her marriage had fallen apart, or if Richard was. She didn't know if she was to blame God for what had happened. She couldn't believe that the man whom she had fallen head over heels for could bring himself to hit her and strangle her. She began to think, and sometimes she would wonder aloud, *'Did Richard really hate me so much that he wanted to strangle me to death? What did I do to him that made him hate me so much?'*

Lydia could also see that it was not entirely her fault, because her husband had chosen to be sly and cunning throughout their marriage. She was still unable to come to terms with his 'gaslighting' effect on her to the point where she had begun to question her sanity. Richard seemed to be thrilled by the impact he was having on Lydia's mental state. It gave him plenty to feed off and he savoured the moments when he heard Lydia talk about killing herself because this gave him ammunition to tell everyone that she was unstable and unfit to raise the children.

She sat alone and began to reflect at what point did the abuse begin and how could she have missed it. It had started with simple things like Richard telling her that he would do the dishes and when she asked him why he hadn't done it yet, he'd say, "I never mentioned dishes today. You're confusing what I said a week ago with today. You're tired. You must be getting old. You're getting quite forgetful." She didn't give it a second thought, why would anyone lie about something as simple as dishes? Then the lies began to escalate. Richard would tell her that he had showed her all his bank statements and she knew that he hadn't, but he was extremely convincing and would get so angry and say, "this is exactly what you do Lydia. You forget everything I say and do and then you ruin the whole evening for everyone. You just want to ruin the peace in the family. Go back and sit and think about the statements that I showed you and then come and talk to me. Stop ruining my life." She was angry with herself that she didn't believe him and she had begun to distrust herself. The blaming began; the monster had injected its lethal poison into her veins.

Lydia now was constantly flooded with thoughts of, 'Did I destroy what I truly believed was a plan of God? What had I done wrong? Where had I failed? How could I have thrown away the man of my dreams, the man whom my entire family thought was the best thing that ever happened to me. He was respected by my family.'

She was ashamed and blamed herself for having being deceived for as long as she had and not telling anyone about the struggles she faced behind closed doors. Lydia blamed herself for tolerating the mental abuse Richard heaped on her every day. She blamed herself for not sharing her pain with anyone and for keeping the strongest face possible. She blamed herself for trying to hold it together in front of her children so they would never see her tears. She blamed herself for being diagnosed with clinical depression for the years of mental, financial, psychological, sexual and financial abuse that was so harrowing that she finally broke down and sobbed uncontrollably in front of her doctor. She blamed herself for telling the doctors that she had overdosed by accident when in reality Richard had threatened her that she would end up in jail and would lose the kids if anyone ever found out that he had forced her into overdosing on anti depressants. Lydia blamed herself because she couldn't cope with Richard anymore. Every other woman seemed to deal so efficiently with their struggles and she was convinced that everyone was coping better than she was. She had seen it in the church, hadn't she, where the pastors' wives seemed so in love with their husbands after so many years of marriage. Lydia had seen the men who seemed to swoon over their wives, and here she was struggling to even be in the same room as Richard. She had never felt more like a failure as a wife and mother than right now. She was so angry at herself for being someone that her husband of ten years clearly loathed.

It was now a month since the incident after the police had escorted Richard out of the house. He had returned home, and Lydia sensed that he was angrier than usual. He seemed colder than ever before to everyone, including the children.

She decided that it was best for the children and the family if she just was upfront with him. She finally mustered up the courage, knelt in front of him and asked, "Can you give up prioritising everything above me and the kids?" Richard simply sneered, "You can't control me."

She looked into his eyes, searching for some assurance that he was simply mocking her and that pretty soon he would say that he loved her and would do anything for her. Wasn't that what he said after every incident of abuse? After every time she was sodomised? After every time he had shoved her? After every incident of falsely labelling her promiscuous so she would have to cower under that indignity? After every antidepressant she took and when he called her crazy? After the many visits to the hospitals caused by the abuse? Lydia was certain that Richard was going to tell her that he loved her, he had to… he always had. She prodded him again, "I need you to make me and the kids the most important thing in your life." He barely looked up from the television and said, "Didn't I tell you that you can't control me? You need to submit as a wife. You call yourself a Christian? You called the police on me for no reason. The Bible says that the woman must submit so you need to first learn how to submit to me."

She felt like she was punched in the stomach. She had just been stripped of her self-worth and felt naked.

She stood up and for the first time, did not react to his cruelty, and knew that he had made her decision easier. She didn't know what she was going to tell her parents. Her parents would not be able to bear the thought that their only daughter had a failed marriage. She began to wonder about the brutal impact her failed marriage would have on them. Would they blame themselves for her failed marriage? Lydia leaned against the deck and as the tears streamed down her face, she thought of her kids. She kept asking herself, 'What am I going to tell my little daughter? My little boy? That I was leaving their father? Oh Lord… didn't my little boy deserve a father figure? Wasn't that the norm? Was it really my decision to make, knowing my little boy would not have his father around him all the time? Would I really be able to step up to the plate and be a mother and father to my two babies? Would they blame me when they realised that it was my decision to leave their father and leave them in a broken family?'

She was walking around in the prison of her mind and rattling the door asking to be let out. Lydia was doomed and trapped by the thoughts of failure. She began to feel the crippling effects of her decision. Her mind stopped functioning and all at once, her mind stopped voicing any opinions. It all just went deathly quiet and suddenly she felt alone in a void. She couldn't bear the silence. She waited for the chatterbox in her mind to start back up again. She heard nothing. She waited for the familiar voice as she told her children that she was leaving her husband. She heard nothing. She waited for the voice as she began her antidepressants again. She heard nothing.

Lydia went in tears to the next safe place she knew… her church. This place was her refuge when things got hard. She entered in tears and looked for a pastor who would help her. Surely her church pastors could save her from this pain. She needed their guidance, their counsel. She was met with an absolute impassive response that left her numb. A pastor simply said, "We do not do marriage counselling here. It's best to look for professional help." She walked back defeated to her car and wondered why was she being met with brick walls everywhere. Was it really because she was a failure, just like her husband had said all these years?

Lydia's mother Anne then met another pastor to seek guidance and advice, but as if to mock her, a few days later he called Lydia and Richard, to his office and told her that she needed to let go of her anger towards him as he had spoken to Richard in private first. That pastor continued, "Lydia, you need to put the children first. Richard has told me the entire story so I now understand everything." That pastor had made a judgement call based on a personal discussion with Richard, but clearly he did not feel that Lydia deserved the same privilege. The mocking continued when that same pastor came home one evening and told Lydia's young daughter Joy that she should ask forgiveness from her father. Lydia was told how Joy would be doomed for eternity if she didn't respect her father. Her daughter was old enough to ask, "Why should I ask for forgiveness from papa? He hit my mummy. Why isn't he asking mummy forgiveness for what he did?" Joy's questions were never answered.

Lydia and Richard were still living under the same roof and that gave her some hope for her marriage. Lydia had gone back to her life with a tiny glimmer of hope that their marriage would eventually work out. She was torn between the abuse in her life and what she had always been taught. Her culture and society taught her that what God unites man must not separate at any cost. She was not sure if she had done the right thing and yet another battle ensued in her mind.

One evening, she heard Richard tell their little daughter, "you just wait and see your mother run off with another man. You don't know the type of woman she is. She'll dump you in a heartbeat." Lydia suddenly was filled with rage at this unnecessary blatant accusation and she decided to speak to Jasmine, her lawyer. Jasmine patiently listened to her and finally said, "Lydia, if you want to save your daughter's mental state, you need to get Richard out of the house. You cannot live in the same roof with your abuser and expect everything to run smoothly."

Jasmine continued, "Lydia, this man's only purpose in life is to leave you drained from all resources, money and emotions. You've tried everything possible to make this work, but now it's time to get him out. You are separated and now you need to decide how you are going to make the most of what's left financially for the sake of your children."

Lydia looked at her lawyer and realised, she was left to fight this battle alone. She heard about how the law shared whatever was left between them, and it didn't take into account the large sums of money that Richard had spent without her knowledge or consent. Jasmine also said, "Lydia, you could choose to fight for it in court, but that means that you would probably lose more than what you would actually gain." She sat hunched over and listened to what little control she had over separating the relationship property. She listened to how she could choose to take it to court to prove the hundreds of thousands of dollars Richard had squandered away or choose to let go and take what she could. Lydia was forced to sell the home she owned with him as the bank froze their joint account which was also the account where her salary went to. She was left with $20 cash, while Richard had a separate account which he constantly replenished to fuel his vices.

Lydia finally resigned to the fact that she would never win against his cunning and manipulation. With hardly any money in her bank account and having borrowed money from her parents, Lydia could no longer afford the long maternity leave she had planned so she was back at work when her baby was six months old. Nothing would prepare her for the extent of lies she was about to uncover.

Jasmine had efficiently managed to get some of Richard's bank statements and very quickly Lydia realised that he was only disclosing what he wanted her to know. There were statements missing and she knew that she needed to take drastic steps. With her heart beating so loudly, she snuck into his office bag and found a USB drive. She was terrified that Richard would murder her if he found her looking through his stuff. That USB drive stored information about his travel and tickets that he had booked. She did something she knew she should have done years ago, she found Richard's passwords to his overseas bank accounts and downloaded the bank statements. Lydia painstakingly sifted through the accounts and went through them line by line and saw the transactions that were missing from what Richard had given to the lawyer. Nothing prepared her for the final humiliation as Richard prepared to move out of their family home.

Lydia discovered that Richard had been staying at resorts and expensive hotels all through their marriage. She stared at the names of the places he had stayed at. He always said that his job was extremely stressful and he needed to work long hours and all along he had been spending time at bars and hotels and resorts when he said he was at work. She looked at the vast sums of money that he had withdrawn and she was stunned into total and absolute silence.

Lydia shrunk as if slapped in the face. She had trusted this man. She had to face the reality that she was the victim of his horrendous abuse because he wanted to silence her. She finally faced the revelation that Richard used the shield of church and holiness so no one would see his horns. She faced the reality that he had cheated on her throughout her marriage. She was humiliated. She couldn't believe that she had been so blind to everything that was happening right under her nose.

She desperately searched for someone to talk to. She wanted to hear words from someone that might comfort her. Again, she was met with a mixture of advice and slander. She heard from some people that she should have been smarter and have left him years ago. Some people said that she should have come to them for help earlier. Others said that Richard was going to come back for revenge. Some said that she was robbing the children of their father. The horrible chatter didn't end there. Others also said that Richard had started telling everyone that their two children were not really his. Lydia understood the extreme low levels he would stoop to, just to take the focus away from his glaring flaws.

She realised, a little too late that she could not convince people about the monster that Richard truly was. Everyone only saw the calm perfect man, but refused to realise that this was what he wanted them to know him as. No one saw the countless hours that he would sulk or throw anger fits when she continued to ask him about where his money was going. No one saw him force himself on her, no matter how much she resisted. No one saw the sex addict that Richard was. There was no way she would ever be able to convince anyone of who Richard truly was as a human being.

She was left with variegated emotions of anger, disappointment and sadness. She sat on her bedroom floor, hugged her knees and wondered, 'Why, why me, why now? Why the children?'

Her emotions finally caught up with her. She was bowled over by the raft of feelings that came gushing from her visceral being. She regretted everything about her life. She regretted her marriage. She regretted having these innocent children and the fact that they were now put through this situation. She regretted life itself. She regretted being born in such a brutal callous society and culture that placed no respect or value on human emotions.

Lydia was angry that she was forced into this marriage just so her family could escape the shame and humiliation of having an unmarried daughter. Where was this society now? What were they doing to protect her from this humiliation? Where was this society to shield her from the emotional carnage? She did not know how she was going to continue in life. She was not sure if she even wanted to continue the fight. Lydia saw the battle and knew that she would never win it.

There was a price that she suddenly had to pay. She was in a place she never bargained for. She sat and cursed her life and cursed God. She never expected to be brought to this place where she would curse the God she loved. She was a deeply spiritual person and she had a strong faith in God and she couldn't understand why God would betray her.

Lydia gave in to her human side and automatically blamed God for everything. She blamed God for her shame. She blamed God for her situation. She blamed God for the pain she was going through. She blamed God for leaving her in loneliness. She blamed God for her life and her agony. She blamed God for the betrayal in her life. She blamed God for being a Christian. She blamed God for being an Indian. She blamed God for the Bible, because after she had finished blaming and cursing God, she immediately felt guilty. Lydia was riddled with guilt because she had grown up with the story of the Bible character Job who did not curse God despite the agony he was handed. She was running in circles with her emotions and she was drowning in guilt and anger.

She could almost hear her ex-husband jeer at her as he had won this round too. She felt that no one was ever going to hear her side of the story. Even if they did, there was no way that they would believe her. Richard had made sure of that. He had successfully convinced everyone that she was crazy and now no one even wanted to hear her out. He had also gone to the extent of looping her extended family to spread more blatant lies about her. She had her own extended family accusing her of ruining the children's lives by overreacting. Lydia was accused of being a home wrecker and deciding to separate because Richard had convinced them that she had another man in mind. She listened to the words spewed from their mouths and tried to justify her decision, but no one listened. She hung her head in shame as she listened to them say that she had brainwashed her daughter to hate Richard. He had isolated Lydia from her entire support group. He had succeeded in making everyone see him as the epitome of holiness and she was the evil home wrecker. He had won for the time being.

She was beaten down in battle at this stage. Everything within her screamed suicide. She didn't feel like she had anything to live for. Lydia looked at her little boy in his crib and wished that he hadn't been born so he never would have to face any of these struggles. She wished the earth would open up and swallow her whole. She had no one around her, no one to turn to and she just couldn't bring herself to be raw before the children. The children didn't deserve to see her, their only strength, break down and weep. She couldn't bring herself to take her life because she saw the innocent faces of her children. She just couldn't bear the thought of leaving her daughter Joy who loved her so much.

Lydia knew that if she took her life, she was going to emotionally scar her children and she couldn't even begin to comprehend the emotions if Joy then decided to take her own life. She battled and struggled with thoughts of setting herself free from this misery. Was it really worth fighting this battle when she had clearly been defeated? She was standing in the battleground, bludgeoned by people whom she trusted. Pierced through the heart by people whom she thought were led by God. Brutally crippled by the God she trusted. Lydia had enough of Christianity. She had enough of the hypocritical church. She had enough of being let down by men of God. She was angry at the church and at God and at everyone and everything around her.

She sat in her room and she thought about the ten years of her marriage. She thought about the medication she was on. She thought about the years of abuse she had endured and she was angry. She was violated and stripped of her self-confidence and her self-worth and Richard had left her naked deliberately. She couldn't face the world in her nakedness.

She began to withdraw from everything and everyone. She withdrew from serving at the church. She withdrew from all social interaction. She withdrew from her friends and swiftly broke much of her social network connections. Her distrust of people grew and took root. Offense took root and in the fertile soil of mistrust and hate, it grew very quickly. Lydia was offended by her church. She was offended by the pastors who led the church. She was offended by the members of her church who did not bother to ask how she was doing. She was offended by the church members who saw her alone with the children and didn't ask if she was okay. She was offended by her ex-husband. She was offended by her family. She was offended by people around her. She was so offended that hate began to grow in her heart.

Her children were the only ones who gave her life a glimmer of hope. She had to tell herself that she was in this battle only for the children. She continued to bottle every emotion inside, every rage, every fear, every insecurity, until she could no longer hold it all in. She needed an outlet, but what? She didn't trust anyone to share her feelings with. She needed to tell someone about everything that was eating her, but whom?

She picked up an empty book and started writing about her marriage, and how the abuse began and she started underlining every red flag that she had missed. Lydia counted the scores of red flags and realised the extent of her naiveté. She began to see her foolishness and the hundreds of chances she had given Richard, and the things she ignored. She couldn't face the truth. She couldn't face the people around her. She was embarrassed by her stupidity. How did she miss these signs?

Lydia suddenly shut down from the world. She walked away from every social situation. She only let her children into that void she called a heart.

Depression hit her like a sledgehammer. She disappeared into a shell. Her emotions left her. She lost her smile, her laughter and her faith in people. She knew that she could never trust again. Lydia was left with nothing except the only constant in her life, something that she didn't want anymore - her Bible. She stared at her Bible and decided to read it one last time before she could rip it into shreds. She opened it and it was excruciating as she began to read it, because she felt betrayed by the so called promises of God. Her mind was now irrational. She wanted to insult and humiliate God. Lydia underlined the promises in the Bible and beside it she mockingly wrote all the betrayal she faced. She wanted God to know that the Bible was a joke and that it was all lies. She was convinced that God really didn't care about the ordinary people.

As she continued to insult the verses in the Bible, she realised that she had been reading it for several hours.

What began as a mockery of God made her study the Bible like she had never done. She began to look for more promises in the Bible to humiliate and this was quickly becoming her familiar place of refuge. Lydia realised that she was so desperate for an iota of respite that she found comfort in the same book that she once hated. She began to find more than just the promises that God had declared, she found the horrific stories of struggle that preceded them.

A conflict rose within as she realised that her issues of depression were never dealt with from the church pulpit. No one preached about her suicidal thoughts. No message was shared about self-harming. All she had ever heard preached was, "Do you not know that your bodies are temples of the Holy Spirit, who is in you, whom you have received from God? You are not your own; you were bought at a price. Therefore honour God with your bodies." (1 Corinthians 6:19-20)

Guilt overtook her as she thought of the times she had been less than a perfect Christian. She had thrown away words that were preached from the Bible, and no wonder God had left her to suffer. She was in a battle with herself. It was a losing battle, but something was unsettled within her. Her thoughts slowly changed course. They no longer were about mocking God, but in trying to understand her faith and the view of Christianity and the church's role in it. She wanted to know what had gone wrong with her faith.

Lydia had been to a refuge support centre and had told her counsellor that she was a Christian and had a deeply rooted faith in God, but at no point in the many sessions she had, was there ever a mention of a church or pastoral counselling that she could tap into. Did that mean that the church had fallen into the trap of the political correctness bucket? Was the church scared to advertise that people who had faith and who were struggling could seek pastoral counselling? Or was the message that Christians were not expected to go through struggles? Was the church too scared of the world? Was the church scared it will lose its members and the snowball effect that would have on the revenue? She had worked in a church setting long enough to have seen this trap in effect.

Lydia knew that the church never really addressed real issues, apart from a few random verses spewed from the pulpit on Sundays. She began to ask herself, 'How could I determine that the church used the Bible effectively then? Was the church really out in the world or were they expecting the world to come to church first to get help? Was the modern day church really preaching about the current issues in the world?' She was thrown into a place and a season in her life that was not her choice or decision. Lydia was faced with making a choice to stay bitter or to look beyond her circumstance, and she knew that the first option was easier.

She had to make the decision to come out of the iron curtains and see herself, scars and all. She had to see her scars and acknowledge that they exist. She had stepped out from behind the curtain and conceded that she was always going to carry those scars, and they would always bring memories of the wounds inflicted. She was faced with the crushing reality of seeing herself as who she truly was and not what her marriage had moulded her into. She had to face the reality of those wounds for the sake of her innocent children. She had to look at the scars as reminders of her survival.

Lydia had to tear away the masks that had now become her. She had to look at her bruised and wounded soul that was scarred like a burn victim. Every raw emotion stung. The pain was too real and she knew that she could never trust again. Lydia refused to believe in love, she refused to believe in victory, and yet, there was something that was keeping her alive.

She saw suicide like the easy way out of this battle, but she knew what the burden of that decision would weigh upon her children. She had to first face her scars. She had to look at her reflection and she couldn't bear to see what looked back at her and at the first sight of herself, she shrunk away. It was barely human. It was a reflection that was filled with anger and seething with bitterness. Her eyes reflected the lack of hope in her soul, but there was still something that wanted her to fight this battle.

Lydia mustered the courage to strip away the layers of masks and didn't recognise this creature that she had morphed into. Only she could remove those masks. She had to start from scratch to understand what her destiny meant. She had to really look at herself as everything she believed in was burning away. Lydia was surrounded by the last, almost lifeless embers of her life, but she felt the fire rising from within those ashes and she knew that…. She will live.

Living meant that Lydia could no longer hide behind her masks. She had to burn away the façade and she stared at her reflection in the mirror. She watched exhaustion catch up to her and she knew she had to remove the layers of masks she had built up to cover her pain. Her masks of humour that covered up her tears, her masks of a stoic front to hide her crumbling emotions and her masks of indifference that hid her crushed spirit. She began to remove them one by one. Tearing those masks off but almost dying inside, she finally came to terms with the truth.

She could finally say that she was a victim of domestic abuse… no, she said that she was a survivor of abuse. She felt the weight come off from hiding the feelings of guilt and shame. The hardest mask she had to strip was 'Lydia'. She no longer needed to hide behind the name 'Lydia'. She was not Lydia.

I, the author of this book am Lydia because I couldn't face the guilt and the shame. I hid behind a name because that meant that I could disassociate myself from my own life. It was easier than actually having to face the pain of knowing that I had been blinded to the abuse. It was easier to hide behind the masks than to face the truth that I had been too stupid to see the signs, but 'Lydia' needed to go. I threw away Lydia and watched that mask burn away to ashes in the remnants of my past, I saw the naked truth.

CHAPTER 5

MY MIND VERSUS ME

I stood in the shower with the water beating upon my face as it perfectly masked the tears. What began as a soft sob, slowly surged into a visceral wail. What a failed marriage actually meant was beginning to hit home… hard. I was beginning to understand what it really meant to possibly go through the rest of my life in loneliness. I was seething with rage at my life veering out of control. I was filled with guilt and anger and the last thing I wanted was anything to do with God, church or anything that remotely seemed Christian. I blamed all Christians and in my mind, they were all hypocrites.

I had to face reality that I was now left alone to work through my pain and growing panic, I distanced myself further emotionally. I refused to acknowledge that I needed help. I soon realised that I still had one mask on. The mask of indifference. This mask covered my loneliness. I quickly began to build layer upon layer of indifference and I was extremely comfortable with it. Indifference meant I never had to face my fears or my loneliness. I began to say, "I'm fine! I'm excellent. Everyone survives. Humans are tremendously resilient. People have gone through worse and survived. I'm only thinking about the kids. Nothing is a priority now. Better to be alone than to be with someone I was not happy with." Classic phrases excused my true heartache. With each excuse I made, I began to add to an already impenetrable iron mask. I began to trivialise my pain.

Surely, I can live with this indifference, because it just meant that no one was going to force me to talk about the pain. I did not want to face what was under the indifference. I loved my perfectly crafted vocabulary that was societally acceptable. No one could hear my soul scream, *'I wish I could just die! I am so lonely, and I'm not sure if this life is truly worth living. Is this misery ever going to end? What on earth have I done to call upon this misery? If I had stayed with him, my life would have become absolute hell but is it any different now that I've left him?'* I dreaded the night-time. The bed only amplified my loneliness. Tossing and turning every night, replaying every incident that my mind could conjure up. The emotional exhaustion was crippling.

I began to slowly come to the realisation that I had no control over my mind. It was playing its best game yet. My mind was in tango with the monster. My mind without warning began to replay my wedding day and the excitement of finding this man. I was shown the euphoria that things weren't all bad as I had made it out to be. Then as if I were slapped, images of the abuse came crashing on me. *'It really was bad, wasn't it? I did the right thing, didn't I? But did I over react? This is what I get for being unforgiving. I could have forgiven him one more time. I chose to be alone and now I want to blame him for my loneliness? He said he loved me. Wasn't that enough? I wanted him to fit my yardstick and he's never going to. I chased away the one important person, who is also my children's father. I must be pleased knowing that I'm supposedly safe but the children had lost a father. Will I ever trust anyone? Every other man is going to come with an agenda, probably more wicked, and how am I ever going to find happiness again? Wasn't it better for me to have stayed with him? Better a known devil.'*

I knew I was no match for my mind. I was crumbling as each word was dealt like a blow. I was crushed under the weight of my mind. There was no escape; I couldn't run from my mind. What was my life leading to? I couldn't shake the words that replayed over and over and over in a rising cacophony. The euphoria of all the wonderful times would begin and it was mere seconds later that I would be dragged down into crippling depression. I could not cope with the peaks and troughs of my emotional turbulence. It felt like a never ending spiral. I was drowning in my emotions and moments where I was convinced that my mind was going to murder me in cold blood. I was terrified to live, but even more terrified to die. I began to tremble at the thought of leaving the house, because I felt attacked by my mind. Anything could be the trigger, a recent physical abuse or a distant memory and the worst attacks were those fantasised by my mind. My mind began to play horrific scenarios. I knew that I had to find refuge before my mind killed me. *The monster was grinning in the shadows of my thoughts.* I was cornered and there seemed to be no way out, and completely overwhelmed with anxiety, I realised I was in no state of mind to talk about it with anyone. I didn't know what was happening to me. Was I going insane? Why was I constantly filled with a growing sense of dread? Was this going to be the death of me? I wanted out. I could not live with my mind any more. I thought about the children, but it seemed pointless. They would be better off without me. They surely did not deserve a mother who was almost insane. I knew I was drowning in anxiety but anxiety was always described as *a choice* and that anyone could just *snap out of it*. I just couldn't seem to find a way out and I felt more like a failure as each second passed. I had lost control of my marriage and now had lost control of my mind.

It was at that point I began to see the face of the monster living inside my mind, and it was powerful. It was an alien and an outside force but knew me better than anyone and its only goal seemed to be to watch me being destroyed. It was the worst enemy I had encountered because it knew me, it was me… and yet it wasn't me. This was as far as I managed to get to analysing this monster. I was desperate to know more about my tormentor as I realised that this monster almost tasted victory because I had not acknowledged its existence and that made it easier for it to go for the kill.

It was the most tormenting point of my life because I could not give this monster a name. I realised I had been married to a monster, but I had no idea that I had been living with another that had made my mind its home. I began to understand every struggle to get out of bed, every slashed wrist, and all the engulfing suicidal thoughts. It was the monster at play. It grew in power by me not acknowledging its existence and I knew I was going to lose this battle. It was me versus my mind; the very mind that was supposed to direct me to my destiny had now become enemy territory.

The battle

Suddenly my *lizard brain* took over and I was slammed with the need to fight… I needed to survive. Every time I thought of the battle with my mind, anxiety would flood my being to the point where I would be shaking or frozen. There was a void where my motivation used to live, where my will to live once lived, but now it had become a vacuum slowly sucking my life out of me. It was easier to give up, but my paleo mammalian brain wanted to fight. I couldn't control either urge and the battle was too big for me. It was me versus myself and sometimes the monster had small victories like when I wrote suicide notes for my family and children, and that made me feel like more of a failure.

I didn't care about who found my lifeless body, hanging or with slashed wrists or the police who found my car with my lifeless body at the bottom of a river, and yet I was bombarded by two thoughts, '*How could you hurt those who love you and what makes you think you're so special that the police would waste their time looking for you?"* The arguments inside my mind were getting louder and all I could hear myself saying was, '*I want to kill myself, but I don't want to die.*'

As ridiculous as it may sound to those privileged to not know this struggle, this is a real battle that I fought every waking moment. Anxiety seemed to be a close companion to my depression, where every tiny decision, even to turn off the light switch, felt like a decision between life and death. This monster seemed to have morphed into a two headed one which was taking over my existence. I seemed to have lost all control of reality and what I could control. Anxiety caused me to worry extensively about the tiniest decision and the disaster that might happen and how I desperately needed to prevent it and depression had made me lose all motivation to live. They seemed counter-intuitive but were also married with the sole purpose to destroy who I was. I will never be able to explain what led my eyes to the Bible. Till this day, I don't believe this was my decision because I did not have enough motivation to fight the monster.

I knew there was something my soul was thirsting for and something inside me seemed to think that the answer was in my Bible. I didn't completely trust that instinct, but I couldn't shake that feeling. There was always a gnawing feeling each time I looked at it. I finally caved in and with an air of arrogance, I opened up the Bible. I believed that my mind was playing games with me, and how could such an old book really have answers to the problems of the modern world? This book was written centuries ago, and in my mind it was irrelevant to today's problems. I had convinced myself that was an archaic book that was a nice to read story and that's where the truth ended.

I had read the Bible before, several times, but this time, I was reading it with mixed emotions. I read through Psalm 23 and everyone, even some non-Christians are familiar with that one, "*The Lord is my shepherd, I shall not want..."* Beautiful! I shall not want... but funnily... I want so much! Maybe I really didn't keep the Lord as my shepherd, which explains why my life seemed so miserable. I continued on to Psalm 55, and what I read there made my eyes widen.

2 "Hear me and answer me. My thoughts trouble me and I am distraught 3 because of what my enemy is saying, because of the threats of the wicked; for they bring down suffering on me and assail me in their anger.
4 My heart is in anguish within me; the terrors of death have fallen on me.
5 Fear and trembling have beset me; horror has overwhelmed me.
6 I said, "Oh, that I had the wings of a dove! I would fly away and be at rest.
7 I would flee far away and stay in the desert;
8 I would hurry to my place of shelter, far from the tempest and storm." (Psalm 55:2-8)

Surely this was not the same man who wrote Psalm 23? Surely this was not King David, who was known as a man after God's own heart. He had just said in Psalm 23 verse 5 that, *"You prepare a table before me in the presence of my enemies. You anoint my head with oil; my cup overflows,"* but he was here in Psalm 55 saying that he was in anguish and he was terrified of the horrors around him. He then goes on to write,

12 "If an enemy were insulting me, I could endure it; if a foe were rising against me, I could hide.
13 But it is you, a man like myself, my companion, my close friend,
14 with whom I once enjoyed sweet fellowship at the house of God, as we walked about among the worshipers.
15 Let death take my enemies by surprise; let them go down alive to the realm of the dead, for evil finds lodging among them." (Psalm 55:12-15)

He was fighting a very struggle with people closest to him and he just wanted to run away. Was this the same King David, the most famous king of Israel? Was he showing his emotional and mental struggles, and yet he seemed to trust in God? I was confused. Wasn't God supposed to get angry with someone who didn't just graciously accept whatever was handed to them? Why wasn't God angry with David? Was there something I was missing here? I went on to read Psalm 41,

⁹ "Even my close friend, someone I trusted, one who shared my bread, has turned against me."

I suddenly was glued to the Bible and couldn't stop reading it. It somehow seemed to make sense to me. I began to be drawn to the meaning of what I was reading. I could relate to this archaic book.

Someone close to King David had betrayed him, and clearly David was not above repeating himself to God about the betrayal he faced. This was controversial to theology which teaches that we should not grumble about our situation. Look at what happened to the Israelites who grumbled about their forty year situation wandering in the desert, they never got to enjoy the blessings God had in store for them (Numbers. 14:21-23). I read through Psalm 55 again and saw the raw anguish that David was crying out with. He was contemplating suicide when he said, *"My heart is in anguish within me; the terrors of death have fallen on me,"* (Psalm 55:4) and the mentality of escapism set into him in verses 6-8, *⁶I said, 'Oh, that I had the wings of a dove! I would fly away and be at rest. ⁷ I would flee far away and stay in the desert; ⁸ I would hurry to my place of shelter, far from the tempest and storm.'* Verse 5 reads, *"Fear and trembling have beset me; horror has overwhelmed me,"* and it showed the real struggle of depression he was faced with. *I understood.* He wanted to get away out of this fight… and he was a warrior and a king… his job was to fight.

I understood that the fight he couldn't cope with wasn't a physical one. David was a master in physical battles, from killing the lion and the bear with his bare hands to his skill with the sling to take down Goliath in 1 Samuel 17:49, so surely he could have annihilated any physical enemy.

What he couldn't cope with was an emotional struggle. Nothing prepares you for an emotional battle. Nothing prepared him for the battle of being offended because he was trying to do the right thing in the eyes of God. Nothing prepared me for the battle that went along with betrayal. I understood and could relate to his struggle. The greatest king in history, with years of training in the battlefield was no match for his own mind.

I was intrigued now. I had read these verses so many times before, but I had to be in a similar season for the verse to come alive for me. Was it any wonder that King David chose to run away from everything and hide? This was not the first time he chose to run. He ran from King Saul, his predecessor. He ran from Absalom, his own son. David, the mighty king of Israel, with the greatest army at his disposal…ran.

I had to go back and read David's history and what he went through to be where he was. The Bible shows that after years of having judges, the people demanded a king. God showed Samuel the prophet that Saul was going to be king, (1 Samuel 9:17) and he fit the description of a king perfectly as he was very handsome and tall (1 Samuel 9:2). Who wouldn't want him as a king? God had chosen well.

Reading further along in 1 Samuel 15:11, God regretted the decision to make Saul a king. All Saul had done was to *try* to kill David and was disobedient. Did that really warrant God's anger? I went on to read David's life and found more than I bargained for. David had clearly not fit into the world's description of a king. The prophet Samuel was sent by God to choose one of Jesse's sons, the youngest being David, to be the next king of Israel. Samuel's eyes automatically fell on Eliab, and he thought to himself, '*Surely, the Lord's anointed stands here…*' (1 Samuel 16:6), because Eliab was tall and was of a similar stature to Saul whom Samuel had anointed as the king of Israel. I then realised that the world has never really changed from making snap judgements based on appearance, and the church was no different.

I began to relate more to the story, because my ex-husband was the epitome of perfection in the eyes of the world, and sadly the church. Imagine how David felt knowing that he was not Samuel's first or obvious choice. I realised the heart of God in the very next verse of 1 Samuel 16:7, *"Do not consider his appearance or his height, for I have rejected him. The LORD does not look at the things people look at. People look at the outward appearance, but the LORD looks at the heart."* I was fascinated that God knew what Samuel was thinking and stopped him right away. Did that mean that God knew what David was really made up of? His weaknesses? His flaws? I read through David's life and saw less than anointed behaviour. Murder, lies and then there was Bathsheba. He killed her husband just to satisfy his carnal desires. What amazed me was that despite everything David did, God still said, "David was a man after My own heart," (Acts 13:22 and 1 Samuel 13:14). How can God regret creating Saul for *trying* to kill someone, but not regret creating David when David actually killed a man to get his wife? The whole logic completely engulfed my small brain.

I guess the answers lay where David repented every time he succumbed to temptation. He knew his shortcoming and was not ashamed to go to God and admit that he had failed to live sin-free. He was not too proud to acknowledge his failure or his flaws. I understood finally, God was not concerned if I was less than perfect, He was only bothered about true repentance that can only come through humility. No wonder He said in Proverbs 24:16, *"Or though the righteous fall seven times, they rise again."* God expects the righteous to fall, and if I was to go into my theological background, numbers have great significance to God, and seven depicts completion. This means that God doesn't mind us falling or failing completely, but He expects that we must rise again. He considers us righteous because we have chosen to find the perfect fall despite faltering. I realised that it was how we were wired. We were born from sin and God acknowledges that.

I did not know how to stop my brain that was running at break neck speed and think about the purpose of it all. The purpose of the dream I had and the purpose of the bruise that was left after that dream. I had to lock myself away from the outside world and just let the emotions overtake me. My emotions overflowed from the mental into the physiological. I was shaking under the roller coaster of emotions. The highs and lows of it shook my being until I had no more tears. The tears streaming down my face meant that I was able to grieve and mourn the death of a relationship. Acknowledging the death of my ten year long marriage also came with its own struggle. I was emotionally drained.

The fragility of my emotional state meant I was forced to mask it at my workplace or in any social settings and that made me afraid to build a social connection with anyone. It felt like I was constantly running from everyone and everything. My tears signified that I had to face the reality that I have no idea about my future and to that effect, no control. My anxiety had now kicked into overdrive. It was crippling to the point that my compulsion was overtaking my life. I knew that though I had left an absolutely horrible marriage, my mental health did not stop deteriorating. I was losing all control of my mind. My only solace was to continue to read the Bible. Little did I realise that freedom lay hidden in these pages.

I continued to read through King David's life and realised that he really struggled with his thoughts. He had run so far and so long that he penned the slow tempo of Psalm 142 that probably is a reflection of his exhaustion. He continued to feel alone, and I related immediately with his thoughts. I realised that I really had no one and was desperate to seek God's face and worship Him, but I couldn't. I wanted to raise my hands in praise and thank God for everything, but with the cares of the world pursuing me and the

enemies catching up with me, I saw myself in David's shoes in Psalm 142.
¹ "I cry aloud to the LORD; *I lift up my voice to the* LORD *for mercy.*
² I pour out before him my complaint; before him I tell my trouble.

³ When my spirit grows faint within me, it is you who watch over my way. In the path where I walk people have hidden a snare for me.
⁴ Look and see, there is no one at my right hand; no one is concerned for me. I have no refuge; no one cares for my life.

⁵ I cry to you, LORD; *I say, 'You are my refuge, my portion in the land of the living.'*

⁶ Listen to my cry, for I am in desperate need; rescue me from those who pursue me, for they are too strong for me.
⁷ Set me free from my prison, that I may praise your name. Then the righteous will gather about me because of your goodness to me."

He was now hiding in the cave and he was unable to praise the very God about whom he wrote Psalm 34:4-5.

⁴ "I sought the Lord, and he answered me; he delivered me from all my fears.
⁵ Those who look to him are radiant; their faces are never covered with shame."

I couldn't comprehend how David fluctuated in his emotions when he penned Psalm 34 and 56 where he trusted completely in God at Gath. But it didn't make sense that he now in Psalm 142:7, put a condition saying that unless God set him free he could not praise.

⁷ "Set me free from my prison,
that I may praise your name.
Then the righteous will gather about me
because of your goodness to me."

Here was King David, hiding in a cave with no one and here I was, sitting in my room with no family around me. I needed to be stronger for my children and my parents. I had a couple of close friends who empathised deeply with what I was going through. I loved my support group dearly and

I know that they loved me tremendously too, but I thought to myself, '*All they can do is say they love me. They really can't help otherwise.*' Yet another battle ensued with my mind. '*Isn't saying I love you enough? Your ex-husband made sure that he cut you off from every support group and destroyed your social network. You should be grateful that you at least have someone around left to help you. You need to stay stronger.*'

I went on to read my Bible in the midst of the voices in my head, trying to find a glimmer of something that remotely represented my life as it stood now. I realised that I had not read the Bible as it was meant to be read. I had been reading it all these years just with my eyes and trying to make it fit into my perception. I needed to engage with God's word differently. I now began reading the Bible with all my senses. I had to hear the story; I had to listen to the side chatter that was going on. I had to listen to the sweet music David played on the harp. I had to see and visualise the places that I was reading about. I had to picture the people I was reading about. I had to smell the story, be it the earthy ground or the faint smell of iron after the bloodshed in battle. I had to smell the sweat that David was probably left soaked in after Saul had thrown the spear at him to kill him. I had to taste the story. I had to taste the tears that ran down David's cheeks as he wept before God.

I had to feel the hard ground that David was kneeling against as he wept to God, the same hard ground that I had knelt on for hours trying to make sense of my life. I had to close my eyes and visualise with all my senses every single chapter as I read it. I had to dive into the actual story that I was reading because that was all I had left and that was the only place that I could escape to.

I was now reading 1 Samuel 21, where David was fleeing from Saul who was determined to kill him. David was left with no armour and the only thing he was handed was Goliath's sword, which probably still had a bit of Goliath's blood on it. With that sword, where does David run away to? Gath. I needed to backtrack and understand the context of the land of Gath. The irony of Gath was that it was the very place where people, including Saul first saw God's hand on David's life when he killed the mighty Goliath. Imagine the strife within the people of Gath who knew that this was the same David who had killed their hero and now was running to the same place with Goliath's sword in his sheath. David had to prove to the people of Gath that he was no longer a threat to them and to save his own life, he pretended to act insane (1 Samuel 21:10).

It broke my heart to watch David, who so proudly spoke of God, forced saliva to run down his beard, pretending to froth at the mouth and scratching the gates to make his insanity convincing. He was struck with such severe anxiety of the unknown that he resorted to irrational behaviour. It must have destroyed him emotionally.

David was terrified for his life, but he realised that he needed to continue his journey as a warrior, and he found comfort by writing ballads. He even set a particular tune to a ballad he wrote while he lived in this excruciating season of his life in Psalm 56. He sang praises in the midst of his fear and he trusted in God completely.

[10] *"In God, whose word I praise, in the Lord, whose word I praise—*
[11] *in God I trust and am not afraid. What can man do to me?"*

As soon as he left Gath, a short time later, David wrote Psalm 142 when he was in the cave of Adullam. He had his family there, but he still felt lonely. David had to put on a façade of strength for the sake of his family but he was dying inside emotionally. David, soon after was surrounded by the worst possible team. The Bible says he became *"commander of four hundred of those who were in distress or in debt or discontented…"* (1 Samuel 22:2).

I felt miserable for David. Can you imagine fighting a ridiculously hard battle, because you had stood up for the truth and then to have the worst possible team of people… those who were in debt or discontented. Meaning, they had no money and they were disgruntled about their own lives. David probably had to break up some fights amongst the men, and I wondered if David really had the time or the patience to deal with that. These men had probably tried their hands at everything and had failed for them to be in debt and discontented.

I reflected at my own situation. Here I was trying to fight a battle that I got thrown in the midst of, and trying desperately to convince even close family members that I needed to leave my husband to protect myself and the children. I never intended for my marriage to end when I placed the wedding ring on my husband's finger, but I also never intended to find out years later that he had been cheating on me all through our marriage. I couldn't seem to convince anyone about his true colours and not once did the thought occur to me that maybe, I should stop trying to convince people.

While I isolated myself from everyone, I was surrounded by people who were struggling. My closest friend had gone through a divorce herself, and her story similar to mine, but I knew that I had to be strong for her. I had to force myself to search for the positives of living, though I was battling suicide myself. I understood David's story at that cave better than I ever had.

David was still running from someone who was once God's anointed and though his own life was at stake, David still chose to spare Saul's life (1 Samuel 24:4). Even cutting off a corner of Saul's robe brought distress to David because he felt he had dishonoured God's chosen. I simply could not wrap my head around the humility that David displayed. Killing Saul would have been easier, and yet David chose not to. The men whom God brought as David's support system were ruthless and it reflected in their language, where every chance they saw they egged David to kill Saul, (1 Samuel 24:6, 1 Samuel 26:8) and it took everything within David to stop himself from killing God's anointed. It was probably God mysteriously teaching David to keep his focus on the higher calling. He was still not above saying that he did nothing wrong, and that God will avenge their relationship (1 Samuel 24:11-13).

It could not have been easy for David to spare the life of the man who was after his own. I imagined David as he probably drew his sword from the scabbard as he raised it above Saul's sleeping head, but lowered it back into its cover because God reminded him of his destiny.

We know that David's brothers were warriors (1 Samuel 17:13) and we need to remember that David himself was a warrior before he was a shepherd. He had been killing bears and lions bare-handed before Goliath made an appearance in his life, so killing Saul with a sword would not have been hard. Plus, we know David's history with accuracy. But, God and ONLY God knew that if these rough men didn't show up, David would never have had his 'mighty men' (2 Samuel 23:8-12) who would lead Him to the throne.

David needed ruthless men who knew how to manage disappointment so that they could keep pushing forward until they reached the destiny.

God saw David's heart and faith and led him to the throne, but it didn't come overnight. It took at least fifteen years for David to become king over Israel (presuming he was fifteen or sixteen when he killed Goliath). So it meant at least fifteen years of running from Saul and yet holding on to his faith.

David realised that killing one giant doesn't mean total victory, because giants beget giants. There is always a new battle to fight (1 Samuel 18:5). There were times where David was seemingly alone on the battlefield, and I related to that. I was alone, and the only thing I had was the Bible and whatever God spoke in it. I was now intrigued by this king who, had he been living in the twenty first century, would have been diagnosed with clinical depression or some sort of mood disorder.

David suffered from mood swings, among other issues and there was no way anyone would have called him a man of God today. I was enamoured. The light began to seep in through the cracks in my darkened soul. I began to see traces of hope. I was sure all hope in me had died, but it seemed like it was beginning to bubble within me. I began to relate to the mood swings, I understood how David, in once stance could humbly say, *"I call on you, my God, for you will answer me; turn your ear to me and hear my prayer,"* (Psalm. 17:6) when he was persecuted by Doeg (1 Samuel 22:18-23) and then quickly his tone changed from a ballad to viciously crying for revenge (Psalm 109:6-15).

[6] *"Appoint someone evil to oppose my enemy; let an accuser stand at his right hand.*

[7] *When he is tried, let him be found guilty, and may his prayers condemn him.*

[8] *May his days be few; may another take his place of leadership.*

[9] *May his children be fatherless and his wife a widow.*

[10] *May his children be wandering beggars; may they be driven[a] from their ruined homes.*

[11] *May a creditor seize all he has; may strangers plunder the fruits of his labour.*

[12] *May no one extend kindness to him or take pity on his fatherless children.*

[13] *May his descendants be cut off, their names blotted out from the next generation.*

[14] *May the iniquity of his fathers be remembered before the Lord; may the sin of his mother never be blotted out.*

15 May their sins always remain before the Lord that he may blot out their name from the earth."

He wasn't being vengeful himself, but was asking God to destroy his enemies savagely. He was subjected to their lies and false accusations and yet David boldly says that he is righteous in God's eyes and his enemies deserved a brutal death. Were such vicious prayers ok? Was God still pleased with David after such prayers?

CHAPTER 6

FAITH TORN BY DEPRESSION

David does a complete backflip and struggles emotionally after trusting God to destroy his enemies. Looking at Psalm 22, the verses show David's languish, he's screaming asking why God has forsaken him. Albeit, this may reflect a discussion about the Psalm prophesying the crucifixion, and Jesus draws attention to this Psalm when He's on the cross, [34] *"And at three in the afternoon Jesus cried out in a loud voice, "Eloi, Eloi, lema sabachthani' Which means "My God, my God, why have you forsaken me?"* (Mark. 15:34) and this forms the basis of Jesus' understanding of depression and agony.

David is crying out because he trusted God and is now forsaken. It begins abruptly with maybe a hint of shock that David cannot believe that God has now forsaken him. He was known as a man after God's own heart. He is in absolute anguish and reading this Psalm with my mind's eye I saw David kneeling on the floor, bent over with his face between his knees and screaming, as he tried to form words amid his cries. He pounds the floor with his fist as he says, "My God, I cry out by day, but you do not answer, by night, but I find no rest" (Psalm 22:2). Maybe he's been shut in his room crying for a few days. He's probably not eaten in a while and is weary, because it's been a few days of not having heard from God and very few people would anguish if God hasn't answered in a couple of days. It has either been longer than a few days or David was used to hearing from God quite quickly. Either way, the struggles keep mounting on David's mind in the midst of God's apparent silence. He raises his hands to the heavens as he cries out, "Yet you are enthroned as the Holy One; you are the one Israel praises. In you our ancestors put their trust; they trusted and you delivered them. To you they cried out and were saved; in you they trusted and were not put to shame."(Psalm 22:3-5)

He begins beating his head and chest as he wailed about his unworthiness, "But I am a worm and not a man, scorned by everyone, despised by the people. All who see me mock me; they hurl insults, shaking their heads. 'He trusts in the Lord,' they say, 'let the Lord rescue him. Let him deliver him, since he delights in him.'" (Psalm 22:6-8)

I visualised David beating the unyielding ground till his fists were bleeding as he was screaming in agony. His voice is probably hoarse and he is oblivious to his surrounding as he now speaks in a cracked voice, "I am poured out like water, and all my bones are out of joint. My heart has turned to wax; it has melted within me. My mouth is dried up like a potsherd, and my tongue sticks to the roof of my mouth; you lay me in the dust of death." (Psalm 22:14-15). David was not ashamed to be real before God. He knew that it was pointless hiding his struggle before his omniscient God.

I'm glad David never described his struggles in too much detail when he wrote his Psalms because that would have given me a reason to disassociate from their essence. I began to wonder if David ever felt that his faith wasn't strong enough to beat his emotional torment. Did he feel the same way as I did? Did he meet people and prophets who saw his traumatised emotional state and whispered within earshot under their breath that this king was losing his faith and might end up as another Saul? Or, did he wear masks to hide his emotional state? Did those words make him sink more into his turmoil? I was excited to read about David's emotional struggle because it meant that when the book of Acts was written hundreds of years later, God still considered David as a man after His own heart (Acts 13:22). Clearly David had done something right, and I was determined to find out what really tugged on God's heartstrings. What did David do to be accepted by God?

The pulpit always saw David as a man after God's own heart and elevated him on a pedestal that someone like me was never going to reach. However the pulpit didn't address the emotional turmoil that led David to become a man after God's own heart.

No one showed the distress that led to destiny.

I went on to look at Psalm 6 and a similar picture is painted. David is groaning in emotional pain and he has exhausted his tears. He's not ashamed to weep and lay his mental state naked before God. David displays his raw emotional nakedness and no matter what the situation was, he was able to be brutally honest with God. He laid bare the battle within his mind before God and yet, it must have taken him a whole lot of inner strength to muster up his voice to sing praises to the same God he felt had abandoned him. I was in awe of this man's inner strength and I realised that David actually found the secret to God's heart. He knew that coming to terms with his weakness was where his strength lay. He realised that his journey was in no means easy, and killing Goliath had not meant the end of his struggle.

In fact, out of his greatest victory came his greatest struggle.

After killing Goliath, David was revered among the people and they even wrote songs to praise him in 1 Samuel 18:7, as they danced, they sang: "Saul has slain his thousands, and David his tens of thousands." Suddenly, the boy who was not the first in line to be chosen by Samuel was exalted by the people. I'll never be able to understand why what happened to David after that, happened the way it did.

The very same Saul, who depended on David to annihilate Goliath, became David's nemesis. Saul also tried to kill David on a number of occasions, and he was brought to a state of absolute humility. His battles didn't end there, forcing him to run to the same place of his greatest victory, but this time not as a victorious warrior. He was humbled before his enemies in Gath, who clearly remembered him as the man who killed their mighty warrior in humiliating brutality.

I was intrigued to find out more about this man David who seemed more human than the pulpit had portrayed. I had never heard a single sermon that dealt with the real man under the armour. David was always portrayed as a mighty warrior, God's faithful servant, and a mighty king and obedient to God… yes, every single one of that is true, but no one spoke of his real struggles.

All the Psalms accredited to David are full of his cries to God. He's crying to God and believing that God was with him no matter what, and yet, he could not see God's hand. I understood.

I struggled with the identical thoughts of distress. I want to believe, I want to be a Christian. I want to trust fully in God for I know that "He has plans to prosper me…" but I don't see His hand at all. I don't see His provision or His grace. All I see is this mountain that I'm speaking to that is just not budging. I'm screaming at the mountain to be removed in Jesus' name and be cast into the sea but it was sneering back at me as it stood firmly rooted in my path. Didn't I have faith as big as a mustard seed? I thought I did. I stepped out of the frame and watched King David step into it. Maybe he could do better. He was screaming at the mountain as well, but from what I'm reading, the mountain didn't seem to be going anywhere either. Did that mean that David had no faith? Did that mean that I had no faith? Was faith even real?

I couldn't understand why God put David on the battlefield alone? How did David still trust a God who seemed to leave him fighting his battles alone? How could David sing praises about the same God who seemingly deserted him? I realised that God working in David's life was not in a clear cut way that I would expect. God's way of working through David's life looked like chaos. God needed chaos to surround David to prove that He is the only constant in any turmoil. David wanted answers and so did I. I wanted to be able to label my struggles and understand if it was God or if it was the devil working in my life, but looking at David's life, I understood that this was not how God worked. God had to be beyond understanding to show His sovereignty.

David was accusing God when he says that God had forgotten him and that he was wrestling with his thoughts (Psalm 13:1-2). He again refers to contemplating suicide as he did in Psalm 55, where he now says in Psalm 13:3-4:

3 "Look on me and answer, Lord my God. Give light to my eyes, or I will sleep in death,

4 and my enemy will say, 'I have overcome him' and my foes will rejoice when I fall."

This verse hit a nerve for me because I understood the desire to 'sleep in death'. I constantly grappled with an inner battle because committing suicide would mean that I was a failure and I still wanted to prove that I was not. Israel's greatest king felt the same way!

It struck me that David constantly had a battlefield in his mind. He didn't quite question God's existence, but he struggled with languishing thoughts of continuing the battle that never ends. He was growing weary emotionally. He was going back and forth because fear and anxiety were crippling him. Wasn't the fear of the unknown crippling me and probably many others as well? The things that I had no control of and yes, I trusted in God and yes, I knew that He was going to guide me and lead me and I would be able to repeat that verse in Psalm 23, "Yea' though I walk through the valleys of the shadows of death, I will fear no evil," but did I really have the courage to walk the talk? I was in a state of constant fear and panic. David somehow claws himself out of his fall into the abyss of depression and manages to pen the last two verses of Psalm 13.

5 "But I trust in your unfailing love; my heart rejoices in your salvation. 6 I will sing the Lord's praise, for he has been good to me."

I asked myself, 'How did David manage to say those verses and was I going over the top in saying that this mighty king was depressed, or at least had some sort of mood disorder?' The Bible doesn't specifically use the word depressed, but as I studied more about some of the circumstances surrounding the words like broken-hearted, turmoil, languish and troubled, I realised that David didn't just suffer a bout of feeling sad or feeling blue. He had full blown mental illness mixed with depression and anxiety.

I went to Psalm 42:5 which reads, "Why are you cast down, O my inner self? And why should you moan over me and be disquieted within me? Hope in God and wait expectantly for Him, for I shall yet praise Him, my Help and my God." Suddenly it all made sense. David knew he was struggling and admitted it to someone he could trust - God in this case. He refused to make excuses about who he was or what he was going through. He didn't go all 'churchy' and say that he was "going to pray about his feelings" and neither did he blame God for the struggles, which has always been my first response. I've blamed God immediately for things that didn't go my way, though I know that the Bible says that God knows better, yet somehow my brain thinks otherwise. I could see the difference now. David didn't spew anger at God; instead he commanded his soul to get a handle on itself and start praising God instead.

David trusted in God so completely, that he ordered his mind to change its thinking.

I had an epiphany then. King Solomon, David's son (or some accredit King Hezekiah) wrote the book of Proverbs and chapter 4:23 says, "Above all else, guard your heart, for everything you do flows from it." This means that King David was light years ahead in his thinking because he was so sensitive to God's heart that he knew that the key to picking himself up was setting his mind right. His son Solomon wrote that verse years after David was already practicing and teaching his soul to get its thinking right. David knew that his soul had a mind of its own and he needed to get it in order. David was not just a shepherd or musician or even a king, he was a prophet in his own right. He knew what Jesus would tell us centuries later, that the world has been handed to the enemy. David knew that the mind is enemy territory because of free will.

That's it! I had finally understood the reason why I continuously had a chatterbox in my mind. God gave us free will when He created man, because we were designed to worship Him in spirit and truth just like John 4:23-24 said, 23 "Yet a time is coming and has now come when the true worshipers will worship the Father in the Spirit and in truth, for they are the kind of worshipers the Father seeks. 24 God is spirit, and his worshipers must worship in the Spirit and in truth." God didn't want us to worship Him because we were forced into it. He wanted us to freely worship Him and only free will could allow that. That's why God was upset with Saul because Saul had chosen to do wrong and had chosen not to repent. That's why God was angered at mankind before destroying them with a flood. They had chosen not to repent. They had abused their free will.

David had it figured out centuries before. He knew that unless he had his mind steered in the right direction, he would never be a man after God's own heart. He had to twist his mind into something it was not naturally used to and that's why his mind fought him. No wonder he struggled to keep his mind constantly in the direction he wanted. David had also figured out the greatest weapon against his mind, because he realised that we cannot win against our mind because the enemy wants God's greatest weapon - free will and obviously he is going to attack the mind.

The New Testament gives us many examples of God's promises, but they always begin with an effort on our part. Free will means we have to willingly want to pursue God and then, only then will the promises be fulfilled. It all began with me exercising my free will in the way God intended. I'm talking about verses like, "Seek and you shall find" in Matthew 7:7 and "Draw near to God and He will draw near to you" in James 4:23. All that begins with me doing something and the enemy is never going to let you do that easily.

David had to act insane at Gath, but he was back again at the same place to gain the trust of the people of Gath. 1 Samuel 27:5-7 (emphasis mine) describes, 5 "Then David said to Achish, 'If I have found favour in your eyes, let a place be assigned to me in one of the country towns, that I may live there. Why should your servant live in the royal city with you' 6 So on that day Achish gave him Ziklag, and it has belonged to the kings of Judah ever since. 7 David lived in Philistine territory a year and four months."

How could this happen, if it were not for God. What was God's strategy?

I began to think about God's battle strategy. The mud in my brain slowly cleared away, and it hit me like a freight train. God was actually on the battlefield in camouflage. God would continue to stand by my side through the battle and reinforce my faith through as many ways as He could, but God will not steer my free will. He will not force me to praise Him in struggles; because that's an action I have to choose with my free will.

God knew that unless David had reached the end of his tether, he was never going to be able to write songs of praise when he faced Goliath or while he was captured by the Philistines at Gath. The enemy knew the breath that God had breathed into man when he created Adam and Eve and he has been determined since then to remove that breath. When he realised he couldn't remove that breath, he tried to violate and corrupt its impact. The enemy knew that the breath is what is in God's mind and the enemy always seeks to violate the purity of it, and the only way that he could do it was by entering the mind as soon as struggles came and then coxswaining the tongue. The enemy knew before it was written in the Word that "Life and death are in the power of the tongue," Proverbs 18:21.

The enemy would do anything in his power to defile it. He knew that Philippians 4:8 tells us to keep our thoughts on what is true, and right, and pure, and to think about things that are excellent and worthy of praise. The only way the devil could control the tongue was by first controlling the mind and that's probably why he's attacking the minds of God's people. Doesn't the Bible warn us of the devil's tactics… he's obviously not going to pick the easiest way to trap us, he's going to pick the most foolproof way. There's no way I can praise God if my mind is feeling defeated. He's tricked us into believing that our mind is defeated and now as a result, we're completely defeated as well.

I was tricked into thinking that I was the only one affected by my thoughts and that no one was as messed up as me. I believed that 'I was messed up in the head' which meant that I was on the extreme of the spectrum of mental health and that there was no in between. I kept telling myself, 'I had faith, I was spiritual, and I believed there was a God, so maybe I was just erratic emotionally because I couldn't make up my mind. I knew there was a God but I doubted Him, which didn't make sense to anyone around me. (Lesson here: Don't share your struggles too early with everyone). How could I call myself a Christian when I didn't trust God all the time? How could I call myself a Christian when I was still suicidal, though I was reading my Bible with renewed fervour? How could I call myself a Christian when I tried to drown my constant screams of 'why God' in the shower?'

I was constantly fed with the lies that had permeated into my society that, if you're a Christian, you should be like God and anything less than perfection gives you a one way ticket to hell. Didn't I know myself better than anyone? I knew that God would never accept someone like me, so maybe I was just fooling myself into thinking I was really saved.

I had reached a point of where I would sit with my Bible open and my thoughts would drift to doubting my salvation. I started saying the sinner's prayer on a daily basis from Romans 10:9, "If you declare with your mouth, 'Jesus is Lord,' and believe in your heart that God raised him from the dead, you will be saved." There's nothing wrong with that, but my motivation was all wrong. I didn't believe I was saved anymore. I began hoping that if I kept repeating it, then it would become true and I could believe it. The devil had a hook into my mind and I saw that I was trapped. My mind was twisted into not realising that verse 10 was my saving grace, which says, "For it is with your heart that you believe and are justified, and it is with your mouth that you profess your faith and are saved." My heart needed to be on board and it needed to be in unison with my words, but it wasn't.

I began to doubt God's promise of salvation.

I first had to face what was going on in my life. I had done something that was considered taboo in my country. I had chosen to leave a man who was an upcoming pastor. I had two children with this man and no one in my society would understand my decision. Unfortunately, this is a secret I still carry and there are family members in India who think that I'm still happily married! If I wanted to allow healing into my life, I had to learn from David. I had to face the reality and accept that this was where I was in this current season in my life.

I had to choose between carrying on lying about my life, or face the reality head on - that I was separated and what society thought didn't really matter. Was I prepared to face backlash? Was I mentally strong enough to listen to people saying that I was the cause of the separation and I should have stayed and that I should have fought for my marriage? Was I willing to listen to people saying that I had given into the devil and destroyed my marriage and God's will is never to separate what He had joined together?

Surely there was a reason why I was going through this season. It was torturous to pretend I did not hear people whisper that I had probably done something atrocious to have deserved this. I had to pretend that I didn't hear people when they said that my actions were causing my children to suffer and that at some point in my life I was going to pay for it through my childrens' lives. The everyday mental trauma was horrendous and now battling the chatterbox was a mammoth challenge. 'They're probably right, you know. They have so much more life experience than you so obviously they're right. What do you know about life? Look at your failed marriage. You couldn't even keep a man for ten years.'

The emotional hurt was absolute torment and through it all, the only option I had was escapism. I had to run away. I needed to keep away from people, even if they were Christians. I had to run and hide and I began to feel safe in loneliness. Little did I realise that the monster living in my head was waiting for just that, it wanted me alone with no support. I battled daily with the demons that haunted my heart. I had to fight off the guilt of my past and the fear that was eating my heart alive. I couldn't, for the life of me understand why I still carried my past in my heart. I asked myself, 'Wasn't I supposed to have accepted the Lord into my heart and 'be saved.' I didn't hear angels sing hallelujah or the sound of resounding bells, but wasn't I supposed to be a new creature? Wasn't this guilt and fear supposed to vanish? Why hadn't it?' My heart was flooded with thoughts of my past continuously. I had to face the judgemental society and I was terrified to even tell them that I had a failed marriage and no idea what I did wrong to deserve this. Why was I in this situation?

CHAPTER 7

MALTA - DO I WANT TO BE HERE?

was still convinced that my struggle with my mental health was completely unbiblical. I knew that David struggled because he was an Old Testament character and I wondered if the issue of insecurity and brokenness was because of the brutality that was in the Old Testament. They were kings, warriors, and men who had to kill and plunder and surely some of the mental struggles needed to be associated with it. Surely the New Testament did not have such gore. It was the time of Jesus after all.

It was time for me to unearth the truth of the New Testament.

The second chapter in the New Testament begins with the same gore, and yet it seemed worse. Herod was killing babies under the age of two because he had discovered that a baby who would become king of the Jews was born. He completely lost his mind and sent his soldiers to break down doors and snatch these male toddlers and kill them brutally, to fulfil a prophecy that was about six hundred years old (Jeremiah 31:15 and Matthew 2:18). Luke as well writes the first few chapters of his gospel in tremendous detail and it's clear that he's done a great deal of research in true doctor form.

Brutality was clearly present in the New Testament. It was not all love and cuddles just because it was the time of Jesus. I began to think of Jesus' crucifixion. Nothing could have been more brutal than that.

I pushed the gore aside as I desperately tried to find the connection between the modern day struggles and this archaic book.

I went on to read about the temptation of Jesus and how He was baptised and the Bible says immediately He was led to be tempted by the devil.

This seemed so similar to what I was facing. I had been excited that I was baptised and that I was now supposedly a new creature and yet, somehow reality was that I was drawn to the same proclivities as before. I couldn't stop asking myself, '*Why am I still not new? Why do I still feel guilty? Why do I still feel miserable? Why don't I feel saved? I'm stuck now in a place where I'm supposedly saved and still feel guilty. In a sense, sometimes I feel I'm in a worse place than where I was before I got saved. I feel like a sinner because I'm saved and feel guilty because I don't feel saved because my mind doesn't feel saved and I'm probably sinning because of that and that means I'm headed to hell. How did I get into this situation? I want out... but I don't think I can get out.*' I felt backed into a corner in this situation that I had ended up in. I was struggling with the demons in my heart and conflicting theories and thoughts and I couldn't get out. I wanted out.

Does anything good ever come out of a situation that you're stuck in? How on earth does this even fall into the 'plan' of God? If God knew that my life was going to be so hard, He wouldn't really have left me in this place to struggle. Surely God just left me to my own devices, because... maybe I had sinned and deserved every bit of this. Maybe God has to let me go through the pits of hell because that's the retribution. Maybe everyone was right; maybe I had to go through this because I deserved it. It was the hardest reality to swallow. The situation was bigger than me, and I couldn't dream of the victory that the stories in the Bible seemed to be talking about. It didn't make sense that I needed to fight a giant bigger than I was and beyond my capacity to handle. It was near impossible to believe that all things were possible through God. I couldn't even change my current state of mind, how was I going to change my entire situation and what was the purpose of this? All I really wanted was to feel free from my mind that was closing in and squeezing the life out of me.

What was the point of getting saved as a teen when all my friends were enjoying life outside of the church and I was left out of everything? What was the point of then becoming a social outcast and being left with no friends? Was I really saved when I started hanging out with people I normally wouldn't, simply because I wanted to fit in and the guilt of it all made me feel like I wasn't a Christian anymore? I could not see my struggle as something I could defeat and I had begun to convince myself that God wanted me to be defeated by this monster just to teach me a lesson. I knew that everyone in God's plan went through something that made sense to them and they had a purpose defined out. They seemed to fully understand the reason of the interruptions in their life and here I was wondering about my life's disruption with the chatterbox that had chased me and now had its lips firmly pressed to my ear whispering about how miserable of a human being I was. I was certain that God would have shown up in my life in all His glory and made everything right if He really had allowed this. He wouldn't have been quiet.

With these thoughts invading my brain, I continued to read through the book of Acts. I had always enjoyed the book of Acts, simply because the book went into great detail of the lives of the early Christians and the point when the word Christian was first coined (Acts 11:26). This book appeared to be a book of lovely stories that seemed to glorify the life of a Christian and how the apostles brought multitudes to the Lord.

I began to read through an intriguing story of Stephen in Acts chapter 7. He belonged to the earliest church and the church was growing rapidly as they continued to serve their communities, but because of the tremendous growth, some of the widows were passed by. This angered a few of the community members and the apostles called the whole church together to help sort this contention out. They set out a strategy so they could cater better to the people and came up with a team of people who would look after mission work and a pastoral team. The mission's team were focussed on outreach and then there was Stephen who did more than just serve. He went above his call and began to preach, calling everyone to the saving grace of Jesus, even those who were not Jews. He was targeted by the Jews who clearly thought that non-Jews were undeserving of anything. They tried to argue with Stephen about what he was teaching, but couldn't stand before the wisdom that God had put in him. So they chose the next best method, lie about him before the council. As Stephen argued his case, the Sanhedrin or governing council could see his face like an angel (Acts 7:15) and after his long speech to them about the mighty men of faith of the Old Testament, Stephen went on to accuse them of having stony hearts and betraying Jesus and putting Him to death. Something in Stephen showed him what was coming and he just looked at the heavens. It was almost like God was showing Stephen the heaven that he was going to soon enter. He let them drag him brutally outside the city and he was stoned. The Bible says he was stoned to death. It was an excruciatingly brutal way to die. The entire mob stood around him as they stoned him and interestingly, Stephen did not fight them or curse them or even justify his actions for his life to be spared. He simply asked that God would not hold this against those stoning him (Acts 7:60). He exemplified Jesus' sentiment on the cross in

Luke 23:34 where Jesus said, *"Father, forgive them, for they do not know what they are doing."*

Aware of the debate about the authorship of the book of Acts and the gospel of Luke, for the sake of this book, I will credit them both to Luke. Luke enjoys writing about the tremendous detail and towards the end of Acts 7, mentions that the men who stoned Stephen laid their coats by the feet of a young man named Saul. It was the same Saul in chapter 8, who approves of their actions to stone Stephen. Saul, for some reason, waited for the death of Stephen before he became the infamous persecutor of the early church. He began to drag people from their home and throw them into prison and scattered the rest. Those scattered because of this persecution, still continued to preach the gospel, despite the horrific brutality they had witnessed.

I needed to study more about this Saul and the history surrounding him.

Saul was a Pharisee and a highly regarded follower of the famous Rabbi Gamaliel and followed the laws of Moses. It was this high point of his life where Saul believed he was fulfilling his life's greatest calling where he was making certain that the teachings by the followers of Jesus were squashed. He ensured that these people were thrown into prison for not following the laws of Moses. He travelled to Damascus so he could imprison more of these followers when suddenly a light blinded him. He heard Jesus' voice and after the blinding light had passed, Saul realised that he could not see. He was stripped of his macho persecutor persona and was left in a state where he needed the help of his men to be led into the very city where he was headed to persecute the Christians there. Saul was emasculated and his weakness left him distraught where he couldn't eat or drink for three days (Acts 9:9).

God, in His infinite grace, sent a disciple Ananias and said that Saul was a chosen vessel. Obedience to God drove Ananias to Saul who gained his sight back and the very first thing that Saul did was to repent of his callous need to kill the Christians. He chose to be baptised and finally managed to eat. Saul spent days with the same disciples whom he had tried to kill and I'm sure it could not have been an easy journey for Paul. He began preaching about the resurrection of Jesus in the synagogues and this baffled the Jews because they knew who Saul was. Saul gained followers who saved his life as the Jews conspired to kill him. He then travelled back the one hundred and fifty kilometres to Jerusalem to where he had initially started his persecution.

This was where Saul had to prove his salvation. Saul had to convince the disciples that he was not an infiltrator who was playing a game with them. He probably was isolated from the wider group. I truly believe that one verse in Acts 9:26 hid a myriad of stories as it talked about when Saul tried to join the disciples, but they were all afraid of him, not believing that he really was a disciple. Saul probably ate his meals away from the wider group and sat silently as the rest of them probably looked at him and murmured and stared.

I began to wonder what Saul did to finally gain their trust. Did he humble himself and offer to do the dishes? Did he offer to clean the floors after the missionary team had fed the local community? Barnabas , one of the disciples probably watched Saul's humility for a few days and then he took him over to the apostles. He explained Saul's encounter with the Lord in Damascus and the apostles let Saul stay with them and the Bible says that the church was filled with peace. The Bible takes a detour in the story and in Acts chapter 10 we read about the vision Peter, Jesus' apostle had with God bringing down all the variety of animals, both clean and unclean according to the Old Testament law on a sheet to ask him to eat them.

This has been explained in many ways, but I think the most convincing explanation has been one that reflects God's heart. The sheet of animals represents everyone who is a Jew or not and God speaks to Peter and says, "Don't keep your own yardstick and decide who is deserving and who is not" *(interpretation mine)*.

I think this goes back to the earlier discussion where Samuel thought Eliab was perfect to be a king because he did fit the yardstick of how a king should look (1 Samuel 16:6). This shows me that God hasn't changed in His thought process because we see in Hebrews 13:8 and John 14:9 stressing that He was the same always and that whoever saw Jesus, saw the Father and Jesus coming to earth didn't make Him any less God. It was another area that God wanted to continually build His disciples in and He continued to teach Peter what it meant to not judge.

God seemed particular about teaching Christians to *not judge*. It was a common theme that seemed to stem from teaching the prophet Samuel not to judge, and now that teaching overflowed to Peter. God seemed very partial to this teaching, to accept everyone and Jesus showed that in everything He did as well. He didn't once judge anyone for who they were or what they did. Maybe God taught Peter this lesson so he would be more acceptable of the people he was meeting... maybe it even included Saul who was struggling to be accepted by the apostles.

Peter was probably the strongest character among the disciples and that made him extremely passionate about the cause of the Gospel. Yet, God in His infinite love, found a way to teach Peter humility and Peter was receptive to the lesson. Peter did make rash decisions but as he grew in maturity in the knowledge of Jesus, he submitted completely to the teaching with obedience.

The Bible then goes back around to the other people who were off on mission trips and there are snippets of the places where Barnabas and Saul were preaching. Shortly after, in chapter 13, we see Saul's name change to Paul to help him associate with those who were not Hebrew. He was a proud and devout Jew (Philippian 3:5) and for him to move to call himself, "An apostle of the Gentiles..." (Romans 11:13) was a great sacrifice of his worldly accolades by associating with those whom he once considered lesser than him. There's something to be said of his journey from Saul to Paul. He fell on the other side of persecution in Acts chapters 13 and 14. Chapter 14:19 shows the instance where Paul was stoned nearly to the point of death. I wonder if, in his mind's eye, he saw the stoning of Stephen (Acts 7). The wheels in my mind turned a little faster. Paul was a proud Christian and preached the gospel with unmatched confidence, yet his past as a murderer did not seem to impact him.

I don't believe that Paul's attitude was completely transformed overnight after his encounter with Jesus. We see evidence of his past nature creep up in a couple of instances, and yet he seemed to be in enough control of those hauntings of his past. Paul's attitude in arrogance (if I can call it that) can be seen in Acts 15:39 where he disagrees with the same man who spoke for him to the apostles. He gets angry and has a heated argument with his friend, but he doesn't let his emotions run amok and jeopardise his destiny. He was able to voice righteous anger without sinning. Paul knew where he stood in the eyes of God. As we travel a little further along the journey of Paul's preaching, we come to Acts 27. Paul is on a journey to Rome to fulfil what the Lord said to him in Acts 23:11, *'where the following night the Lord stood near Paul and said, "Take courage! As you have testified about me in Jerusalem, so you must also testify in Rome."'* He was going to Rome, just as the Lord promised, but not as he hoped. He was not going with accolades; he was going as a prisoner.

The promises of God don't always look like what we expect.

While onboard as a prisoner about to stand trial before Caesar for preaching the gospel, Paul warns the crew, in Acts 27:10, *"Men, I can see that our voyage is going to be disastrous and bring great loss to ship and cargo, and to our own lives also."* No one listened to him, instead, they continued on their route through Crete. Then the storm began, first as a gentle south wind, gradually becoming the tempest that would force the crew to throw their precious cargo overboard. The storm lasted fourteen days and Paul's attitude (maybe from the years of being highly respected as a student of the great Rabbi Gamaliel) was not above telling them something to the effect of, "I told you so... " (Acts 27:21), but he brought his attitude in check immediately by speaking the plan of God over them. Paul had refined himself in his walk with God to acknowledge his human side but to not stay in it. Paul didn't complain or moan because this whole thing was clearly not working according to his plan. Though what he was in the middle of was not part of the plan, Paul's faith was not subject to the storm.

Faith must not be subject to a storm. Faith doesn't stop the storm, it teaches you to overcome it.

Acts 27:25 laid out what faith should mean: *"So keep up your courage, men, for I have faith in God that it will happen just as He told me."* Verse 35 of the same chapter reflects what faith actually entails: *"After he said this, he took some bread and gave thanks to God in front of them all. Then he broke it and began to eat."*

It's one thing to say that I have faith - it's a whole different battle when that faith needs to be exercised by giving thanks when clearly there's nothing around to be thankful for. Their ship was destroyed, but they had survived.

Nearly three hundred of them survived the raging storm and landed in an unrecognisable and unfamiliar land and it was only after they reached there did they discover the island's name was Malta. The wheels in my head were spinning quicker than before now and I slowly began to understand what that story was telling me.

The map below shows the destination intended by the crew and the dotted line shows where they ended up.
Credit Google maps emphasis mine.

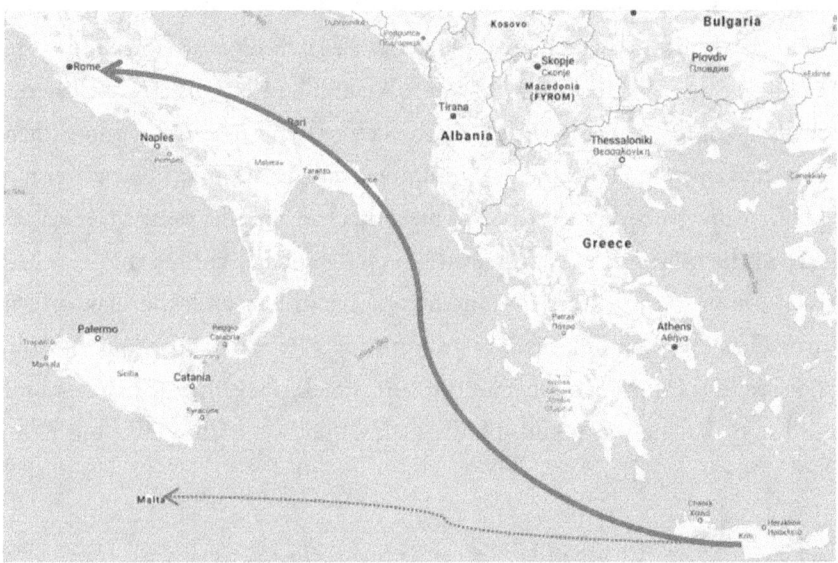

Malta was not very significant when compared to a magnificent city like Rome but it was significant enough to be mentioned in 10 verses of Acts 28. Those ten verses carried some of the most crucial lessons of the Christian battlefield for me.

Paul was in a place that he was not interested to be in and this foreign land was full of islanders who probably didn't speak the same language and some translations referred to these people as barbarians (KJV). Apostle Paul and the few hundred men had walked out of the shipwreck, soaking wet and emotionally distraught by the uncertainty around them. They were surely in no emotional state to handle the natives who initially were probably concerned about this boatload of shipwrecked strangers. Paul acknowledges the kindness of the people and clearly, he is not one to just sit and enjoy being served, and in his time of emotional and physical weakness, he gathers up firewood to light the fire. The drama at Malta doesn't end there; it's a matter of minutes before a viper, drawn out by the heat of the fire latched itself to Paul's hand. I'm wondering if he yelled suddenly alarmed by the sight of the snake, but the snake itself latching onto him didn't seem to bother him. While the snake was still dangling from his arm, he listened to the people, probably including the crew saying this was a punishment Paul had to endure because he was a murderer (Acts 28:4). They went on to say that maybe he was destined to die at sea but since he escaped, it was his fate to die by a snake. Paul ignored the judgemental chitter chatter which is common to the nature of human beings, and he shook the snake off his arm. They watched closely for a long time (verse 6) and when they did not see him crumble or succumb to the attack, they changed their minds and said that he was a god. How quickly they went from labelling him a murderer to a god!

The situation you are in can change how people perceive you.

Paul didn't let either their ranting or praise phase or deter him. He carried on as humbly as he could and was called to the house of Publius who was Malta's chief official. He stayed there for three days and found Publius' father terribly ill. Paul prayed for him and he was healed. Immediately, everyone who was sick on the island lined up to receive healing.

    This story reveals the raw core of Christianity. The reality is that Paul wanted to get to Rome because that was the promise of God, and he didn't want any deviation from that plan. He was angered by the fact that the crew did not listen to his guidance, because he had heard from God. He ended up in unfamiliar territory and I'm sure Paul asked God to remove the storm he was trapped in the middle of. Paul's situation was not unlike Jesus' who Himself told God, *"Father, if you are willing, take this cup from me; yet not my will, but yours be done."* (Luke 22:42). The decision made by the crew led him to be stranded on an unknown island. He most likely didn't know the people around him nor the language. He was frustrated and angry at where he was and the story just seemed to get worse from there. He tried to find some comfort by getting warm, and then he was bitten.

I'm sure we can all relate to where we've ended up in a situation where we're hurting and shaken by the storm that's tossed and thrown us around, and yet we've somehow survived the storm. Surviving the storm can sometimes mean that we look for comfort when we're still weak and struggling to get up on our feet and we get bitten in the same place where we sought comfort.

You can get bitten if you seek comfort from anything that is not God.

Paul probably knew it before it became a social media trend - to not let others decide his worth. One day the people around him are in awe that he survived the storm and then the next they cursed him for bringing the storm upon himself. Jesus experienced the same thing.

Hosanna one day, crucify Him the next.

I learnt from Paul that sometimes we end up in unfamiliar territory like Malta, sometimes not by our choice or decision.

Our destiny doesn't change just because our course changed.
Out of great inconvenience can come great learning.

I think the great take away from this story is slaying the myth that bad things only happen to bad people because I think Malta is a story of God's master plan. I firmly believe that God is a master jigsaw puzzle player and having read this story, I realised that God had intended for Paul to heal and save a whole island that he might have missed if the crew had listened to him and not sailed from Crete. They might have escaped the storm but missed a miracle and we would never have had the ten verses. Sometimes, our best thought out plans are interrupted. It seemed fantastic that Paul had to push aside his own struggles to see the greater need that was at Malta. God had a lesson in these ten verses for me. He needed me to look beyond my shackles and see that I had survived and that there are people in a worse place than I am. People needed to see my situation as a blessing in theirs.

Out of life's greatest interruptions comes God's greatest work.

CHAPTER 8

PEAKS AND TROUGHS OF FAITH

I seemed to have all my answers lying in front of me. Everything seemed to make sense in the Bible. Yet, I was buried in my thoughts so deep that I just couldn't escape them. I couldn't stop the monster that had made my mind its home. I couldn't run away from my mind. Surely I was not the only one stuck in the spectrum of mental illness. I went back to the Old Testament because it felt like mental illness had come alive in the twentieth century. Looking back, I was pretty sure that if David had struggled with depression, there must have been others. How did the heroes of faith in Hebrews chapter 11 stay heroes of faith? I needed to find out a bit more about some of them.

Uncertainty versus Faith
I was curious about Moses. I had grown up with the story of Moses who parted the Red Sea and who led hundreds of thousands of Israelites out of Egypt and slavery. The Bible adds the unpleasant details of slavery and

the escape from it, and visualising the situation made me see more than what my Sunday school had taught. Moses, the man known for his faith, doubted and God was patient with him. He asked God, "*What if they do not believe me or listen to me and say, 'The Lord did not appear to you'?*" (Exodus 4:1), and yet God didn't strike him down. The verse in Hebrews 11:6 has been twisted beyond recognition, "*And without faith, it is impossible to please God because anyone who comes to him must believe that he exists and that he rewards those who earnestly seek him.*"

The latter half of the verse is not emphasised as much as it needs to be. God rewards those who earnestly seek Him, which means that God wants us to be serious in our purpose of seeking Him. We must be true in our feelings toward Him and even if we are unsure about what He's doing; He does not strike us down for being truthful about those emotions. He knows what's in our heart and hiding it from Him is not wise. God understood Moses' feelings and He helped Moses through the next steps. He took Moses through baby steps to increase his faith and we could see Moses' faith being restored in the next few verses. He did everything that God told him to, whether it was turning his rod to a snake, or making his hand leprous (Exodus 4:2-9).

Here was a man who was adopted by Pharaoh's daughter (Exodus 2) and who was brought up with the same privileges as Pharaoh's family. When Moses spoke, obviously as a member of Pharaoh's family, he got the attention of the people he spoke to. He was skilled in words and action (Acts 7:22), and I was curious how a person who was considered skilled in 'words and action' could tell the Lord, in Exodus 4:10, "*Pardon your servant, Lord. I have never been eloquent, neither in the past nor since you have spoken to your servant. I am slow of speech and tongue.*"

Was Moses lying to God? Or did he slip into fear after he killed the Egyptian and refuse to talk to anyone? I could only make an assumption, but I was more curious why God seemed angry with Moses but didn't punish him. Instead God said that Moses' brother Aaron, who was three years older than him (Exodus 7:7) would be his mouth (Exodus 4:14-17). Moses had fled Egypt in fear (Exodus 2:15) and stayed in Midian for forty years (Acts 7:40) and he was eighty when God visited him (he was forty when he fled Egypt according to Acts 7:23). I figured Moses, the great orator had lost his confidence when he fled from Egypt and that's why God was angry because Moses had retreated into a shell and forgotten who he was. God seemed upset that Moses had let fear steal his confidence. God was not cruel in His anger. He instead supported Moses by showing Aaron's eloquence because He understood the trauma Moses had gone through for forty years.

God wanted Moses to stay in line with his destiny and He did not want Moses to battle with his confidence. Moses regained his strength, both emotionally and physically to ask Pharaoh to set the Israelites free.

Then God told Moses that He's going to harden Pharaoh's heart (Exodus 7:21). I wonder if Moses' confused exclamation was, "Really Father? That's just not cool." Poor Moses had to stand in front of Pharaoh who blatantly refused to free the Israelites and instead made their workload harder. It must have crushed Moses' spirit and I know if it were me in Moses' situation, I would have rued being the messenger of God, which is precisely what Moses did in Exodus 5:22-23. Moses returned to the Lord and said, *"Why, Lord, why have you brought trouble on this people? Is this why you sent me? Ever since I went to Pharaoh to speak in your name, he has brought trouble on this people, and you have not rescued your people at all."*

God promises that the Israelites would be delivered and it was an encouraging spiel but shortly after, God again says that He has hardened Pharaoh's heart. I don't think God intended for any mortal to understand His reasoning, but I simply believe that He needed to give Pharaoh many chances to see His power and also it was to teach Moses to trust in God fully. Moses still didn't trust God because in verse 23 he says, "*You have not rescued your people at all.*" I empathised deeply with Moses and yet, his faith was encouraging. He chose to stick with God rather than leave and run and he still continued to see and perform the miracles God had empowered him with.

The next few chapters must have increased Moses' frustration but he didn't complain anymore. He was being moulded into what God intended. It took ten plagues for Pharaoh to finally set the Israelites free.

God needed Moses to see Him in all His glory so He could reveal His wonders among the unbelieving (Exodus 11:9). There was drama throughout the exodus from Egypt. The Lord didn't choose to use the shorter route to bring them to the Promised Land. Pharaoh suddenly decided that he had made a mistake and set off in his chariots to bring his slaves back. Moses was met with cries of the protesting Israelites and the Lord simply told Moses to move forward despite what was looming behind them (Exodus 14:15). The Israelites were on foot and the Egyptian army was gaining fast. God told Moses to stretch out his hand and the Red Sea would part. I imagined Moses gazing into the distance and wondering probably why the sea didn't split immediately. It took all night for the winds to part the sea and maybe the sea had begun to move back right under Moses' feet as he gazed into the distance waiting. What astounded me was that the Egyptians trusted in the miracle that God had set aside for the Israelites, as they rode through the parted Red Sea.

God even makes an avenue for the wicked to ride on the coattail of the blessings of the righteous.

Eventually, the Egyptians were destroyed as the parted Red Sea closed on them. It had to take a mighty miracle for the Israelites to fear and trust God. The story flows to God continuing to provide for the Israelites, but they were not satisfied and continued to grumble. I believe that God's decision to make them wander for forty years in the wilderness is part of testing their free will. God wants us to use our free will to worship Him in spirit and truth and nothing else will do. Moses continued to bear the call of God on his life and all the while teaching the next intercessor who was Joshua, but even Moses was brought to a point of despair.

What troubled me was Moses' despair had nothing to do with his own personal walk with God, but it was purely because he was bothered by the grumbling by the people. He was also troubled by the anger of God that was rising and he said in Numbers chapter 11 verses 11 onwards, [11] *"He asked the Lord, 'Why have you brought this trouble on your servant? What have I done to displease you that you put the burden of all these people on me?* [12] *Did I conceive all these people? Did I give them birth? Why do you tell me to carry them in my arms, as a nurse carries an infant, to the land you promised on oath to their ancestors?* [13] *Where can I get meat for all these people? They keep wailing to me, 'Give us meat to eat!'* [14] *I cannot carry all these people by myself; the burden is too heavy for me.* [15] *If this is how you are going to treat me, please go ahead and kill me—if I have found favour in your eyes—and do not let me face my own ruin'."*

Moses was allowed to let his emotions loose. I would have thought that Moses' rant filled with frustration would have angered God but He appreciated Moses' honesty. He manages to calm our human mind with a solution and there's nothing more father-like than that.

Depression versus Faith

I slowly started to make my way through the Bible and came across the story of Elijah. I saw this amazing prophet who probably related to me more than anyone else. I was amazed by the fact that he had called a drought on the nation and God listened. God not just listened to him but also sent ravens to feed him, which in my mind was the worst possible choice. Think about it, ravens are one of the greediest birds that ever flew on the face of the earth and to have them feed someone else unselfishly was unheard of. Didn't that prove God's battle strategy even more to me? He will use the most unlikely means just to confound the human mind and steer it in the way of confidence towards Him. Elijah didn't just call the drought, but he trusted God so deeply that he even arrogantly asked Ahab who was Jezebel's husband (1 Kings 16:31), *"How long will you waver between two opinions? If the Lord is God, follow him; but if Baal is God, follow him."* (I Kings 18:21).

Elijah was called troublemaker just four verses earlier and yet that didn't seem to faze him. He dramatically said that he was the only prophet left who followed God but Baal seemed to have four hundred and fifty as well as four hundred of Asherah's prophets. He says that whichever God answers by fire is the true God and he watched the prophets of Baal call on the name of their God from morning until noon. That's when Elijah's amusement peaked and he began to taunt them. He asks for a competition between the Lord and Baal, and what competition would be fun without a little trash talking? One Bible translation says he even trash-talked Baal's bowel movement along with Baal probably out on vacation. It was almost evening as Baal's prophets continued to scream for their god to respond by fire and at that point, Elijah had had enough.

The more times I read that incident, the more I longed for the same confidence that Elijah had in the Lord. He built an altar and his confidence in God even made him dig a trench around the altar and pour four jugs of water three times, that's twelve jugs of water. Some would say he tested God by drenching the altar to prove a point, but to me, Elijah didn't doubt God for a second and neither did he waver in what he knew God was capable of. He couldn't wait to prove to everyone about God's awesome power. He simply stood there and with a voice that resounded with pride in his God, asked the Lord to answer with fire, and God did, burning up the water and all. I can almost see Elijah grinning and smirking at the prophets of Baal who fell down and cried that the Lord was the true God.

Then Elijah flips and suddenly displays a completely different personality, where he tells some unknown people to seize and slaughter every single one of Baal's prophets. Elijah was in no means humble, except before God where he then decided that the drought needed to end. He sat with his head between his knees while he sent his servant to go and look toward the sea (1 Kings 18:42-44).

I had to visualise this. He probably waited for his servant to manoeuvre the rough terrain to go look toward the sea. What astounds me is the obedience of Elijah's servant, because he probably had no idea what he was looking for, except maybe assuming that it had something to do with rain. The obedient servant rushed back as quickly as he could and each time Elijah heard, "There is nothing there", he sent him back through the rough terrain again. (1 Kings 18:43).

Finally, it was the seventh time when the servant came back with a report of seeing a cloud as big as a man's hand. I believe that the Bible places great significance on numbers and it might only be seven times, but seven according to God, is a number of 'completion' and it might also be symbolic of Elijah telling his servant to keep going until the miracle was complete.

Elijah refused to give up and he understood the significance of God answering in His time. He wasn't ruffled in the slightest when God didn't answer straight away like He did with the fire. The moment he heard that there was a small cloud, Elijah knew what was happening but in my mind that had no significance. He was so attuned to God's spirit that he knew that the miracle was here, and he took off like lightning. I wonder if his servant was amused at Elijah's reaction to the little cloud or did he follow Elijah too?

Elijah had already told Ahab that there was going to be heavy rain, though there had been no rain for over three years. It seemed like nothing was happening in the spiritual, but Elijah knew the significance of the cloud. Elijah understood Hebrews 11:1 before it was written, *"Now faith is the substance of things hoped for, the evidence of things not seen," (NKJV).* He didn't wait for the rain to come, he just had to hear about the cloud before he hitched up his cloak and ran around forty kilometres overtaking Ahab's chariot. I longed for faith like Elijah. He never gave up on God. He didn't need to see the miracle to believe.

Then suddenly, the next chapter shows an unexpected change in Elijah's faith. Jezebel the Phoenician queen heard from Ahab about how Elijah had slaughtered the prophets and she was furious. She sent a messenger to let Elijah know that she was going to kill him (1 Kings 19:2). Elijah suddenly was filled with fear. Jezebel could have killed him at that point, but all she did was employ scare tactics. She knew that she could not touch the Lord's anointed but the enemy employs the same tactics. He knows how to mess with your mind and this was exactly what Jezebel did. The same Elijah who taunted the prophets of Baal was engulfed in fear. Fear choked his faith and it gripped him for over a day (1 Kings 19:4). Fear doesn't need more than a few seconds to destroy anyone's emotional stability, imagine having fear grip you for more than an entire day. Elijah began to run and reached Beersheba, which was about a hundred kilometres away.

Fear made him run further than his faith did.

It must have crippled him and fear clearly disillusioned him into seeing the beast bigger than it really was. Elijah saw his life under threat. Fear had wiped his memory clean, he completely forgot about the fire that just fell from heaven. Elijah had an anxiety attack that left him crumbling at the foot of the broom tree. He just gave up. He gave up on everything that God had called him to do and be. He collapsed under the weight of fear. He struggled with the very thought of living. He cried out for God to kill him and I visualised him screaming for death. His throat was probably burning and his voice hoarse from crying out to God. He was desperate. His faith hadn't changed from the time he left for Jezreel. He just was overcome with fear and he was blinded to his faith. His persona took on fear and anxiety. He was physically exhausted, but that paled in comparison to his emotional and mental exhaustion. He knew that he was going to die, either by Jezebel or by his fear of her. He began to plead with God to take his life and he questioned his self-worth. The very same mouth that had brought fire from heaven was proclaiming his worthlessness before God. He felt like a failure probably because the fire from heaven had brought no revival. I empathised with Elijah; I knew what it meant to feel like a failure. I too had run after a cause and had failed miserably. I imagined the humiliation that Elijah would have been subjected to. His own servant must have wondered what was running through Elijah's head.

Here he was one moment praising God for rain and the next instance he was crippled with fear. He was practically paralysed by fear and that's the interesting turn in Elijah's story. One of the tell-tale signs of depression is feeling alone and verse 10 of 1 Kings 19 shows, "*I have zealously served the Lord God Almighty. But the people of Israel have broken their covenant with you, torn down your altars, and killed every one of your prophets. I am the only one left, and now they are trying to kill me, too."* He began to feel alone and whether that was true was irrelevant at that moment to Elijah. He just saw himself alone in this battle with his fear.

God's response to Elijah's fear was the best part of the story. He was not angry with Elijah. He was not upset or even disappointed. I was taught that God would be disappointed when He saw His children's faith shaken, but nothing was further from the truth. He saw the weakness that was embedded in mankind's flesh. It amazed me that God didn't choose to appear to Elijah to give him advice or even send a prophet to explain the next step Elijah was expected to take. He simply smiled at His prophet's passion for the city and sent His angel to comfort Elijah. He knew what was needed to bring immediate relief for Elijah… comfort food! That took me to thinking about how much God really cared about His people. He knew that at that point Elijah didn't need advice… he needed sustenance. He let Elijah sleep. God was concerned with Elijah's physical state because He knew that Elijah needed to strengthen his physical being before he could get emotionally and physically strong.

I needed to see for myself that God cared not just about our spirituality but he deeply cared about us as a whole. He knew that unless Elijah was physically strong, he would never be strong mentally for the next phase of his journey. God allayed Elijah's assumption that he was alone, in verse 18 of the same chapter, *"Yet I reserve seven thousand in Israel—all whose knees have not bowed down to Baal and whose mouths have not kissed him."* God felt it necessary to dispel that fear of loneliness immediately to build Elijah's strength and courage.

I began to think about how I was taught that I should never be fearful but be forever filled with faith. This teaching was so embedded in my mind that it became a struggle for me to talk to anyone about my fear. The fear, as irrational as it may seem to someone else, seemed very real to me, but I couldn't tell anyone about it. Especially, since as a Christian I was supposed to have the power of heaven and with Christ in me, how could I fear? I have constantly been crippled with my own fear because Biblical teaching has been contorted to somehow force us to live like perfect creatures. Everytime I spoke about my fears, the verse in 2 Timothy 1:7 has been thrown back at me, *"For God has not given us a spirit of fear, but of power and of love and of a sound mind."* The teaching of that verse was restrictive that I wasn't allowed to express any fear and that meant that I had to bottle every fear within my mind.

This was not how God intended us to live. He never wanted any one of us to live in fear, but He doesn't mind if we are crippled by fear. He's there to lift us up and help us with our destiny. He's there to be our strength in our moments of fear.

God watched Elijah hit rock bottom emotionally and mentally and He knew exactly what Elijah needed. Elijah ate what the angel set before him and fell asleep again. Again the Lord sent His angel to bring Elijah food and water and Elijah was not shocked to see the angel again. He knew that God was in control, but somehow his faith had been overshadowed by fear. That did not make him any less loved by God. God was in this relationship for the long haul. He was going to get Elijah's faith up one way or another and this time it was with food.

God appeared to Elijah and gently asked him what he was doing. God doesn't interrupt Elijah but He patiently listened to Elijah vent his frustrations. He then directed Elijah to get his focus back on God and to begin seeking the Lord's face. God let Elijah share his emotions and then as any parent or good friend would do, He doesn't let Elijah stay in his sobering emotions. He guides him to the place that would provide respite. It was the same place where Moses regained his strength. It took Elijah forty days and nights to reach a place called Horeb which some believed to be the same place as Mt. Sinai. Elijah then experienced mighty signs, earth-shattering winds, earthquake, and fire and amazingly the Lord was not in these mighty signs. It is important to know God well enough to realise that He is never in the obvious.

He is never in what we think He is capable of.

He is capable of sending mighty winds and earthquakes but He was in the gentle whisper, which would have been barely audible if Elijah was trembling with fear at the mighty signs. Elijah seemed to now be at peace at the signs of God and had absolutely no fear because he heard the whisper amid the burning embers in the fire's aftermath. How easy it would have been to miss that whisper. Amid the chaos, Elijah heard God ask him, *"What are you doing here, Elijah?"* in 1 Kings 19: 13-14. If Elijah didn't hear that gentle voice, we probably never would have had Elisha or even Elijah's ascent to heaven. Elijah still managed to get a whinge in, which God again patiently listened to. This time God gave him specific orders to go back to where he came from. God wanted Elijah to face his fears and return to those seven thousand Israelites who had not bowed to Baal.

Elijah had to struggle emotionally and battle with his mental state to be able to recover from it and to go back and defeat his fear for the salvation of others. I constantly think about the many of us that are in the same situation. Does God have a greater destiny waiting for us that is being held back or crippled by fear? I realised that God had a destiny for each of us and He was never going to give up on us. God founded the *Pray Until Something Happens* (P.U.S.H.) trend before it was cool. He probably would have tried to get Elijah's attention in a number of other ways too if Elijah hadn't heard or obeyed. He was not going to give up on Elijah's destiny and I think we need to constantly remember that's how God works. He's always in the still small voice and that small voice led Elijah to his destiny.

God had to remind Elijah that he had a destiny to fulfil and that the destiny was conceived in heaven, so obviously it was not going to be an easy journey. Elijah went back and faced Ahab and Ahab practically spits out at him, *"So you have found me, my enemy!"* (1 Kings 21:20) and Elijah found his courage again. He was able to again prophesy punishment to the same people whom he ran from.

Elijah had grown in confidence again and he understood the road he had to take to come to where he was at. He understood what had happened to him and he knew that each milestone in his life signified a lesson he had learned. We see that a few chapters down in 2 Kings 2, Elijah and his faithful servant Elisha were walking from Gilgal (which was the place the Israelites camped after crossing the Jordan in Joshua 4:19 - 5:12). More importantly it probably signified where God had set his people apart as we read in Joshua 5:2-9, and no matter what Elijah said, he could not get rid of Elisha. They went to Bethel (House of God) - probably to signify when God proved his existence to Elijah just like He did to Jacob in Genesis 28:16-19. They then went to Jericho which was the most iconic place. It was where God taught His people the power of faith, which was where Elijah realised that he needed to go back to Ahab.

Theology teaches that numbers hold great significance to God and when God told Joshua to walk around seven times and with seven being the number of completion, I believe God was telling His people to keep at it till the destiny is fulfilled (Joshua 6). Then they went to the Jordan which symbolised the mighty miracle at a flood-swollen Jordan River seen in Joshua 3:15-16, where the Jordan is at flood stage all during harvest. Yet as soon as the priests who carried the ark reached the Jordan and their feet touched the water's edge, [16]*"the water from upstream stopped flowing..."* It is also the same river that Jesus would later be baptised in Matthew 3:13. Elisha was probably taking all this in and he needed Elijah's faith to build his own.

I began to reflect symbolically that the struggle in my life was Jericho because that's where the victory of persistence lies. In the midst of the struggles of every day, when the cares had beaten me down and where I knew that I was never going to win this battle, could I still believe that the walls were going to come down?

I had to get across Jericho to be at the place where I could look at the glory in Jordan.

Was God so clearly showing me that I needed to persistently fight in Jericho until I had the victory? Was that His battle strategy all along? As simple as it seemed, God taught Joshua the key to being a military genius on the battlefield. It almost seemed like common sense, and it seemed like a no-brainer. I had to persist on, and any sane person would persist to come out victorious… right?

CHAPTER 9

THERE WERE MORE

T hese stories started to get me excited about the Bible. These were not just ordinary people like me who were hit in the face with depression or struggling with anxiety. These were leaders of mighty armies who led hundreds of thousands to battle and these same men had fallen victim to a wavering mental state. The stories of these warriors struggling with their mental state weren't just limited to the likes of men in battle like Moses, David or Elijah.

Anger vs Destiny
The Bible speaks to our mental state when we have been wronged and the emotional turmoil that it brings. Too often the anger inside eats us from within. The self consuming question we so often ask ourselves is why and what did we do to deserve this? Genesis 34 speaks of the rape of Jacob's daughter Dinah. Jacob was probably the Biblical poster child for being cunning and sly and maybe getting his own back with his father in law Laban (Genesis chapters 29-30). I imagined the agony of Jacob knowing his only daughter was violated and now the same man wanted to marry

her. Jacob looked past the trauma that his daughter had gone through and even if he did take her state of mind into consideration, he had aged in his years and probably had resigned to the fact that he was now reaping for his sins. His sons Simeon and Levi however were not going to just sit around and accept this. They were so fuelled by anger and rightfully so, that they ended up hatching a cunning plan to humiliate and kill the man who defiled their sister. God did not see their actions as just and that bothered me because I'm sure as human beings we would have done the same thing. Both Simeon and Levi are cursed for their violence and anger, which by their father's curse that was put on them, shows that they had groomed their anger for years. Reading Genesis 49:5-7 showed me Jacob's curse on their anger where he said, "'*Simeon and Levi are brothers— their swords are weapons of violence. ⁶ Let me not enter their council, let me not join their assembly, for they have killed men in their anger and hamstrung oxen as they pleased. ⁷ Cursed be their anger, so fierce, and their fury, so cruel! I will scatter them in Jacob and disperse them in Israel'.*"

I was extremely distressed reading these verses. How was I expected to just accept the injustices I saw? Was that even possible, and was that even right? How was it acceptable to God that I just stay quiet at all the injustices? This was an aberration to my thought process.

Albeit, I was not going to use my anger to cripple bulls for sport, but I did let anger fester and that led to un-forgiveness and there was no worse internal infestation than that. Harbouring un-forgiveness is the worst injustice I could inflict upon myself. It began to pervert the course of God-ordained destiny for me. I saw this in Deuteronomy 33, a little ahead in the journey of the sons of Jacob, where Simeon is the only one who misses out on Moses' blessing. Why was Simeon cursed but Levi blessed? He was in the murderous plot too. Something had changed in Levi's intrinsic murderous and violent nature. I think it is found in Exodus 32:26-29 where the sons of Levi truly repented of their nature and knew that in order to fulfil the destiny God had in store for them, they had to prove that they wanted to be consecrated before God. The tribe of Levi were never born as priests. They had to make a public declaration amid the sinful people they were surrounded by. That was where Moses in verse 29 said, *"You have been set apart to the LORD today, for you were against your own sons and brothers, and he has blessed you this day."*

The thing with God's prophetic word is that the Levites were still scattered in line with Jacob's prophetic words, but only this time God used them to become priests and spread the name of the Lord in the places that they were scattered in (Deuteronomy 33:10). Moses was a Levite too (Genesis 46:11 and Exodus 6:20) which might reveal why he shared the same proclivities of a violent nature and why he had to work through them in complete humility.

Simeon did nothing as atonement for his actions but Lévi was humble and did not justify his actions toward his sister's rapist. It was far from what I thought was acceptable. I thought God would understand that I was trying to do the right thing and play my part in bringing injustice to an end. Surely if God saw that the inclinations of my heart were righteous, He would understand my anger, right? The Bible says no such thing. God tells us that we are entitled to be angry, but He gives us no permission to sin as recorded in Ephesians. 4:26, which says, *"In your anger do not sin."* That potentially means not to take justice into our own hands. I never expected the Bible to speak to me on so many levels and I began to understand the gravity of the challenges these people were faced with.

If I go back to the story of David that we saw earlier, he was angry with Saul and could have killed him, but he only cut a corner of Saul's robe. He knew God's heart so deeply, that he immediately regretted this act that was harmless on the outside, because he knew that his anger had made him take justice into his own hands (1 Samuel 24).

Fear vs Destiny

I had to move on from the sobering reality and look at the Bible again. I came across the story of Joshua. Here was the story of a seemingly humble second in command to Moses, but a scary warrior. Having read the book of Joshua, there is a darkness surrounding his character because it takes a dark character to be able to impale people as part of a normal battle ritual (Joshua 8:28). Joshua was a man who was loyal to Moses and who trusted God completely. He was also among the few who tried to keep the Israelites from cursing God and turning on Moses (Numbers 14:24 onwards). Joshua's humility to follow Moses gave him entry to the Promised Land. I believe that Joshua understood kingdom principles and that pleased God. Joshua began to watch God constantly help and prosper the Israelites and I believe that like any one of us, he became complacent in his faith. Joshua was constantly surrounded by violence and bloodshed and there was a season where he went looking for a fight, albeit unprepared.

He went to war with the city of Ai which was much smaller than the city of Jericho where he had just won the battle. He lost that battle. The defeat at Ai shook him. It happened just after the massive and very surprising victory at Jericho. He fell from a massive victory to a shameful defeat and immediately the hearts of his mighty warriors melted in fear. The bloodthirsty and brave Joshua tore his clothes in shock, fear and a plethora of other emotions. He lay before the altar with his elders until the evening. His prayer was filled with fear, both for his and his people's wellbeing and for the name of the Lord. He was filled with fear of being wiped out and destroyed and for some reason, the Lord waited until the evening to respond to him. Fear is not a word I would associate with Joshua, but even this mighty warrior was fearful of his destiny. He let Joshua vent his emotions. He didn't interrupt Joshua's tears, because humans can make impulsive decisions when they're emotional. Joshua needed to be clear-headed to hear the voice of God. Joshua wasn't immune from facing an emotional turmoil. He realised that he couldn't take God for granted and seeking God's guiding hand was key to moving ahead to his destiny. He also probably realised that defeat in one battle doesn't mean the end. He did go on to vanquish the city of Ai soon after. He did not take his victory or his emotional state for granted after that. God knew the toll that a life of battle and war would have on Joshua so He reminded Joshua three times in one conversation to stay strong. God says *"be strong"* to a man who was a warrior and as a warrior, Joshua was probably physically intimidating, but God was not concerned about the physical state of Joshua. He repeats Himself to Joshua and I know it must be important if God had to tell a trained warrior three times to *be strong and courageous* from Joshua chapter 1 verses 5 to 9. It was getting exceedingly clear that God was speaking to Joshua's mental state.

I began to see how important it was to God that His warriors had to be strong. If I was to go by what the Bible spoke about our lives as being one of constant warfare, then I deeply believe that God wants our mental state to be warrior-like as well.

The story of struggles didn't end there. There were more strong men who had to learn what it meant to guard their mental state.

Struggles vs Destiny

Jeremiah, as you may know, was a prophet who wrote a few books in the Old Testament. He was known as the weeping prophet. He was faced with struggles trying to carry on what God had destined him for and that left him depressed. He was so overcome by grief and the weight of the struggles made him write, *"Cursed be the day I was born... why did I ever come out of the womb to see trouble and sorrow and to end my days in shame?"* Jeremiah 20:14-18. I understood why he felt like he did. I'm sure I'd be curled up in a ball crying out in agony too if there were people out to kill me every single day. What I didn't understand was, if God chose Jeremiah to be a prophet who would bring His word to the nations, why would he choose someone like Jeremiah? Had it been the twentieth century and had Jeremiah not been the famous prophet of the Bible, I'm certain his own church would have called him weak of spirit. He would have been asked to step aside and let someone more courageous and brave take that place because Jeremiah didn't have the courage to carry on God's word. Why would God choose someone who seemingly hated his calling because he felt like a constant failure? Wasn't I supposed to believe that if God chose someone, they were automatically equipped with the strength of heaven to be able to carry out what God wanted?

God thought otherwise. He just wanted someone who was true to what the calling was and God could then move His chosen from victim to victor. He understood our mental state and He was not going to let us succumb to the victim state where we would crumble under the attacks of the enemy. He was going to take us through the journey and each battle we are faced with is a lesson for us to move higher up the warrior ranks.

Unforgiveness vs Destiny

Let's look at another character, and boy was he a character! Jonah and the big fish was a story pretty much the staple at every Sunday school. Here was a man whom God asked to go to the city of Nineveh, which was the capital of ancient Assyria and tell them about the love of God. Jonah heard the voice of God and without saying a word, he ran away. He wanted no part of this. He ran to Tarshish which was about four thousand kilometres away from where God asked him to go. He chose to run away than have anything to do with God's calling. Jonah was again caught up with fear because the people of Nineveh were known for their brutality and at some point; Jonah's city was also ravaged by the Assyrian attacks.

Many pulpits have preached about Jonah falling asleep in the bottom deck of the boat and not being bothered about the fate of the ship he was on. I believe that Jonah knew what he was getting himself into by running away from God and the weight of that upon his shoulders left him emotionally exhausted and he slept.

The story goes to when the ship's crew heard that he had disobeyed God and decided to throw him into the sea. Jonah then got swallowed whole by a giant fish.

He knew what God intended and he cared about God's plan which I saw reflected in his prayer inside the belly of the fish (Jonah 2). He wrote about God's merciful hand from inside the fish that he was stuck in for three days. He did not seem too deterred by the fish; instead, oddly he was on a faith high and couldn't stop praising God. He went back to the place where God had directed him to and got the entire city to repent. He experienced the many peaks and troughs of emotions through this journey.

At this point, a mentally stable person would feel elated and proud of the work accomplished, but not Jonah. He was clearly struggling with some mental health issues, and I'd venture a guess to say bipolar. His emotional state plummeted without any warning. His mental state waxes and wanes and he completely lost the plot. He was angry at God and angry at himself for having done God's will. His emotional state jumped from praise to punitive. He began to shake his fist at the heavens (or so I'd like to visualise it) and was deeply angered at God's compassion. Various translations of Jonah 4:1 shows the extent of rage that Jonah flew into. He lost complete control of himself and began to speak unreasonably. He declared that he knew God would be merciful to this city and that's why he ran away to Tarshish. He was furious at God for saving these people and he almost felt like he wasted his journey to Nineveh and that his time in the belly of the fish was wasted. He began to downplay his effort and question his purpose.

His anger at the city of Nineveh repenting may have come down to his self-worth. He didn't see God commending Jonah's efforts to obedience, instead, all his distorted mind saw was that his efforts were wasted and God didn't fulfil what He said He would do. He knew God as loving and forgiving but he wanted God's punishment. He didn't seem to value his own efforts. Jonah could not see that the people repented because of his obedience to God. He only looked at what he proclaimed at Nineveh which was destruction (Jonah 3:4) and he was so blinded by his inherent belief in God's character. He didn't see the destiny, but only saw the one-shot scene of the whole story. Again, the patience of God and His compassion flows through and He patiently explains to Jonah that His intention was never to see people perish. God realised that Jonah was angry to see horrible sinners shown mercy, especially those who had wronged him and his city. God reveals to Jonah that it was God's intention to deal with un-forgiveness.

I began to wonder about the many teachings I've heard about the harsh God of the Old Testament and the kind love of Jesus in the New Testament. The story of Jonah shows me that God hasn't changed and it was true that anyone who has seen Jesus has seen the Father (John 14:9).

Pride vs Destiny

Job was an interesting story I knew I had to read again. I felt like I could relate to Job. In my mind, I was trying to do the right thing for the family and my children and for no reason, I seemed to have come into the firing line. Reading just the first few verses showed me Job as a model man in society, such a model man that the devil couldn't bear it.

God even boasted about him to the devil and almost seemed like God put Job in the firing line. Job very quickly lost his children and his possessions and before long, he had lost his health and his body was covered with boils.

Job didn't stop praising God in his struggle and I cannot imagine anything worse than losing your children and yet Job says, *"Naked I came from my mother's womb and naked I will depart. The Lord gave and the Lord has taken away; may the name of the Lord be praised,"* (Job 1:21). Job said something extremely profound in chapter 2 verse 10, *"Shall we accept good from God, and not trouble?"* Job had figured out the key to kingdom principles, something that Jesus explicitly explained centuries later in John 16:33, *"In this world you will have trouble. But take heart! I have overcome the world."* Job's three friends surrounded him trying to support him, and for seven days they sat silently because they didn't have words to comfort him. Job bore his suffering in silence, like most of us do because no one really understands the struggles that loom over us. When he finally broke his silence, he cursed the day he was born and wished he never existed. Towards the end of chapter 3, he's unable to speak and probably only groaning in pain and grief. His support network stood with him in times of trouble, but gradually their theological conformist thinking began to show. His support network of friends became anything but supportive. I believe that we need to be careful whom we choose as our support group or friends. Friends who stick by you just to watch when you suffer and pour an air of self-righteousness over you are more dangerous than enemies.

Job listened to his friends tell him that he deserved his fate. They start in chapter 4 by telling him that righteous people don't usually suffer, so surely Job must be unrighteous. At some stage in the next chapter, his friend Eliphaz tells him that sometimes God corrects us to guide us, but it's clear fairly quickly that Job's life was an exception to the rule that God punishes the wicked. He thinks about Job's suffering and finally declares that Job is a wicked man and reading through chapter 22, his friend is berating him for being a wicked and selfish person who did no good. Job doesn't accept their accusations and calls them *"Worthless physicians who are liars…"* (Job 13:4).

Job, in the next few chapters has come to the conclusion that despite his righteousness, God has left his side (Job 29:1-6). Elihu, out of nowhere speaks in chapter 32 where he is angry at Job for magnifying his righteousness instead of God's. After he talks for five chapters, the Lord speaks. There have been several arguments about if Elihu was right or if he was too harsh on Job, but the essence of it was that God knows what He's doing. He needed to allow the pain on Job so that Job's inner thinking could be fixed. Job doesn't argue with Elihu like he did with his other friends and chapter 42:6 shows Job repentant when he says, *"I despise myself and repent in dust and ashes."*

I believe the pride of righteousness had set into Job. This was a clear failing and God needed to remove it from Job and that is found in chapter 33:17, *"to turn them from wrongdoing and keep them from pride…"* The picture Elihu paints of God is one of a saviour who allows pain and hardship to remove that speck of blemish on ourselves so that He can see Himself in our lives. We see that in chapter 42:7-9 where God restores double to Job. He saw true repentance and understood that these men were lacking understanding in the revelation of who God really was.

I think the biggest revelation was that you don't have to be a spotless righteous person, just striving to be conscientiously righteous is seemingly enough to find favour in God's eyes. He knew Job was not spotlessly holy and he had certain areas to be worked on, but that earned him God's certificate of approval of *"Blameless and upright, a man who fears God and shuns evil,"* (Job 1:8).

That in itself was enough for me to know that God really doesn't care about the level of perfection we are at, but just the effort in striving to get there. The other comforting fact was that sometimes we need God to sort some of this out for us, some of the stuff we don't even know we're struggling with. If something comes at us from the enemy, then we know that God allowed it and He's able to use anything to turn it around to build us. If something was permitted by God as a test, He's still going to use it to build us ... so either way, God's got us!

CHAPTER 10

REALITY AS GOD SAW IT

The battle as you know it is unique to you and only you can pick up the weapons you need to fight the enemy off. The support network you've built can only pick you up after you've been injured or they can tell you what you should have done after the attack comes. They cannot fight the battle for you and no one knows the timing of the attack better than you.

Remember, the church cannot fight your battle. When the spear is thrown at you, the church cannot change the course of that spear, you need to be strong enough to do it. No one is going to fight your battles for you. The church is in the battle together, but it is eventually our own battle to fight. The rest of the army will come around and help you when you're wounded.

Don't fight the battle expecting that someone else can take the hit for you. The enemy is after you and knows your weakness and your vulnerabilities when he attacks. Remember, the church is made up of human beings, who need your support just as much as you need theirs. I think the true test of Christian maturity lies when there's been an offence on the battle field. From experience, this is truly the most potent weapon the enemy uses to eliminate the support network because a lonely man makes for an easy target. It's similar to how the abuser operates. The enemy's battle strategy is to make sure that you're offended by your own team so when you're isolated in battle and attacked, you have no one to carry you from the battlefield to nurse the injuries.

What is an offence? It's when you've been unjustly wronged by someone, and that someone could be anyone. The truth be told, it's extremely painful when it's someone close to your heart, but the pain can be just as searing when it's from the church community and especially the leaders of the church. The pain can cut you like a knife. How you react here can either make or break your mental health. The Christian walk was never designed to be easy and no one, not even God said it was going to be easy. How could it be easy when Jesus said, *"... I came to give life, and life more abundantly,"* (John 10:10). If you ask anyone, and they don't have to be a Christian to tell you that life has its ups and downs. Now imagine a life, already fraught with ups and downs, but with Christ to give you a more abundant life. What's that telling me? The ups and downs are going to have higher peaks and deeper valleys, so we were pre-warned a few millennia ago.

Now, I'm not saying that we should completely disconnect from the church. We do need the people in the church; we do need our flaws and their flaws to cause a bit of friction. It's the only way we're going to get stronger in our faith and walk with God. We need to acknowledge that each of us has a strength that the other person needs and that strength has to rub off to sharpen each other.

What is critical to understand is that we shouldn't judge each other for what they bring to the battlefield. The battlefield is not a place to be offended. A soldier in battle, hurt by his own army, would understandably be extremely upset. But it's important to understand that the offence was probably not deliberate, and even if it were deliberate by some soldiers who went rogue, we need to keep our sights on the destiny. It does sound easier than the reality. To let go of an offence is probably the hardest thing I've had to do. It seemed harder to forgive my abuser because he was Christian. The wounds caused by well-intended words from people who thought they were trying to fix it cut me like a knife. "Can't you forgive him? Have you forgiven him yet? Have you considered getting back together; he's your husband after all. You might need to stop over reacting."

The well-meaning words came off as inconsiderate and apathetic and left me asking myself, "Why am I being victim blamed and shamed?" I found my Bible and realised that I was missing an important key. *Why do I keep going back to the Bible?* Simple answer.... I had nothing else left. No other book or person strengthened me, and believe me, I tried to find my strength from so many sources. I tried to drink desperately from oases that turned out to be mirages. They never had any strength to give, in fact, they seemed to be draining me of my reserves. I was let down every time. Then I began to read the Bible, and at that point in my life, I really had no expectation from it. I knew what it said because I had read it before, and I knew that the Bible hadn't changed in centuries. It was in this time of absolute mistrust of everyone and everything and loaded with offences from everyone, that I found out what it truly meant to hold on to an offence.

I pictured the battlefield in my mind. When a warrior or soldier is injured, the army in the Christian battlefield needs to send at least one other warrior to support the injured soldier. If the wounded soldier is offended by the support soldier for whatever reason, it can cause more hurt and then the support soldier becomes another wounded person or casualty and they, in turn, require another support soldier. The phrase 'hurting people hurt people' sums up this context. This has been a leading reason why entire churches have been taken down. *Offended soldiers.* I'm not saying that it's wrong to be offended, but carrying that offence is not only detrimental to the health of the church community, but especially our own mental health. In more blunt terms, it means that it's an extremely unrealistic expectation if we think that we're never going to be hurt by another Christian. That's just the way of the battlefield. We are going to be hurt but I need to acknowledge that there's more depth to the hurt we experience. We are going to be hurt but we need to realise that it is the way the cookie crumbles because Jesus was there first. He was hurt by the very mankind He formed out of nothing. He was accused of being demon possessed (John 10:20). He was betrayed, not once, but three times by Peter who was the same person who declared, *"Even if I have to die with you, I will never disown you."* (Matthew 26:35) and (Luke 22:54-62). I can't even begin to fathom the betrayal Jesus felt when He turned back to look at Peter.

Then He was betrayed for thirty pieces of silver (Matthew 26:14-16) by another one of His chosen ones. It must have crushed Jesus' heart to have gone through betrayal upon betrayal during his short ministry time. Jesus prepared us for everything He went through when He said, *"Remember what I told you: 'A servant is not greater than his master.' If they persecuted me, they will persecute you also. If they obeyed my teaching, they will obey yours also,"* (John 15:20). I don't think we should really be surprised, given that we've seen the reality of human nature and if we're going to put our trust in human nature, we have to be prepared to be tremendously disappointed.

Jesus probably was the best example to show that hurting people don't have to hurt other people. We don't have to *take it out* on anyone because we're hurt. We can actually *let it go* and yes, I've harboured hatred for longer than I've liked or needed to but I've also seen the negative effects it has had on my life. The people who have been hurt by my hatred and anger have not been the people who hurt me; instead, I've ended up hurting people closest to me - people, whom I didn't intend to hurt. The anger and bitterness had me wrapped in its vile clutches.

I was trapped and the thoughts of being wronged flooded my being and I was being thrown into the abyss of my brain, which was an extremely dangerous territory. I lived in an endless roundabout of emotional distress. I would spend countless hours every day thinking about the brutality of the ten years of abuse and how I should have left my marriage sooner. Then I would beat myself up about why I didn't get out sooner *because I didn't see the red flags.* Surely a person with half a brain would have seen the red flags? *Maybe I didn't even have half a brain, isn't that why I was abused for ten years?* Maybe I trusted too much, which made me more naïve than I usually was, or at least thought I was.

These thoughts were wrapped in wondering why and how cold-hearted abusers could get away with everything and for how much longer. It seemed absolutely fine to have these thoughts randomly, but it became crippling when my body stopped functioning as these thoughts became like vultures circling my every waking moment. These thoughts began to destroy my will to live because they didn't let me see beyond the negative. I was blinded by the negative thoughts that, like the Israelites I couldn't see the Red Sea that was parting beneath my feet because the negative thoughts wanted me to focus on the monstrous Red Sea and not the miracle (Refer Exodus 14). I couldn't see the miracles that were helping me through everyday.

Let me use another example to explain the importance of why I had to keep my eyes on my destiny. Joseph was a character from the Old Testament whose story did not make sense to me. I'll say that a little differently - Joseph was a character from the Old Testament whose story did not make sense to me... until now.

I watched the life of Joseph documented in the Bible at the age of seventeen when he was tending sheep. His father Jacob loved him the most because he was born in Jacob's old age (Genesis 37:3) and clearly Jacob could not keep his favouritism a secret, because Joseph's other brothers hated him when they found out (verse 4).

Silence didn't run in the family, because Joseph had a dream and he immediately told his brothers about it, who hated him more because the dream was interpreted as everyone bowing down and submitting to Joseph. That didn't stop Joseph from sharing another dream, this time with his father as well, who also got angry. That's when the rest of Joseph's brothers got jealous and the name calling started and the plot to kill him (verses 18-19).

Not long after that, he was thrown in a well that had no water because two of his brothers, Reuben and Judah were the lone voices who didn't want to kill Joseph. Joseph, for no fault of his own except for speaking his dreams to the people whom he should have been able to trust, was then sold to the Ishmaelites. Who were these people? Going back a few chapters, Joseph's great-grandfather Abraham had decided to take his destiny into his own hands to get the promise of God quicker. God had promised Abraham a son (Genesis 15:4), but Abraham, like most of us do, decided he had waited long enough, so he and his wife decided that Abraham should father a child with their Egyptian slave Hagar. The child born to Hagar was Ishmael whom the Lord still blessed (Genesis 16:10). Ishmael's descendants were those who took Joseph from the well and sold him in Egypt. Here was another story of someone trapped in a situation he had no control over. Yet, Genesis 39:2 tells us that the Lord was with Joseph, no matter the circumstances, so much so that the Egyptians saw the Lord's hand on Joseph and the Egyptians flourished as well.

Now, as experience teaches, life never stays on a high, and not even a Christian life. We must remember that it is a very real battlefield and there is always something out there that will make you take your focus off eternity. It was the same with Joseph. Very soon, the Egyptian official's wife wrongly accused Joseph of attempted sexual assault and the cloak he left behind while he ran away from her grasp was used against him. There was no way Joseph could prove himself and obviously, Potiphar who was the Egyptian official would be inclined to believe his own wife's version of what happened, so Joseph got unfairly thrown in prison. Yet, the Lord was with him, but that didn't mean Joseph escaped prison or that prison never happened for Joseph. He had God by his side, yet he had to go through prison.

The true test of faith lies when your circumstances don't change.

Joseph was then imprisoned and after some time, a couple of men who were fellow prisoners came to him asking Joseph to interpret a dream. The interpretation of the dream worked out exactly as predicted and resulted in one person getting beheaded and the other man tasting freedom. Joseph requested that he be remembered when the person was freed so that Joseph could get out of prison as well, but the request was promptly forgotten (Genesis 40:23). Joseph was again dealt with the harsh reality of betrayal. His situation began with his trust betrayed by his own brothers and then being betrayed unintentionally by someone whom he pleaded with to help him get out of prison.

Watching Joseph's life showed me that God had something to teach him. I was brought up and taught to feel sorry for Joseph and that may be true because he was subjected to unnecessary torment in his life, but God still found a way to teach him something in that distress. If the man told Pharaoh about Joseph and had Joseph been set free because he interpreted the dream, then the glory would have gone to Joseph.

Joseph had to learn humility, which seems to be the main lesson God wants to teach us. Genesis 42:8-9 shows the point where a little bit of Joseph's past and possible anger seemed to have crept back in.

[8] *"Although Joseph recognized his brothers, they did not recognize him.* [9] *Then he remembered his dreams about them and said to them, 'You are spies! You have come to see where our land is unprotected'."* His human side showed because he chose to indulge in the drama, possibly partly due to the fact that they might not have believed him if he had said it straight up that he was Joseph whom they sold.

I think despite the story that ensued over the next several chapters, Joseph knew what God had done for him and because he was in a comfortable place with the trust He had in God, he said, *"I am your brother Joseph, the one you sold into Egypt! And now, do not be distressed and do not be angry with yourselves for selling me here, because it was to save lives that God sent me ahead of you.... So then, it was not you who sent me here, but God. He made me father to Pharaoh, lord of his entire household and ruler of all Egypt."* (Genesis 45:4-8)

He had believed that God had ordered his steps and I believe it was because he realised God's love in his darkest moments. God didn't stop Joseph from going through the journey of the pit to the prison, instead, He used that to exalt His name through Joseph's story. I think that made the story of Joseph so compelling. It was brilliantly detoured by God to bring Joseph's dream to a fantastic realisation. It could not have been easy, but I visualised God at every step, silently pleading with Joseph to just trust Him. It surely meant something when God refused to remove the circumstances from Joseph's life. I'm sure Joseph kept asking God to remove the situation that was so uncomfortable for him, but God didn't acknowledge it, because He knew there was a throne while Joseph was still in prison. God kept building Joseph's faith through the pain and agony because He needed him to climb to the throne so he would value the life lessons he had learnt. But most importantly, if Joseph did not go through his story, he could have never said, *"... because it was to save lives that God sent me ahead of you."* (Genesis 45:5).

Joseph could see God with him in his struggles because his faith in God only grew stronger. Only God could use the suffering Joseph encountered to mould a leader. Joseph was a leader who not only saved Egypt from the famine that was destroying the rest of the world but he was a leader who saved his own family who had betrayed him. His own tremendous suffering led his brothers to repentance. Joseph learned to be compassionate to others, despite struggling himself (Genesis 40:7). He asked the cup bearer and the baker, who were fellow prisoners with Joseph, why they looked troubled. He had learned empathy in his trials. I think those are some of the most important lessons that God intends to teach because He modelled it. Jesus modelled love while He hung on the cross dying. There is nothing more important to God than getting His children to live as He would, and He understands that there is no way that we could achieve that to perfection, but God needs to see us trying to live how He designed us to live.

Through the book we've seen His plan and thinking, and the brilliance of how He looks at the puzzle pieces that are strewn before Him.

Only He can look intently at each piece and fit it in the most perfect place in a way that never seems logical. I had to work through my emotions before I could understand that my brain was no match for the maker of the Heavens and the Earth. I had to learn submission and when I didn't know how, He taught me, maybe not in a way I liked, but I learned it nonetheless. It reminded me of what I do on a daily basis at work and how much I talk about 'getting to the root causes' when I run meetings. I began to make an unnatural, yet actually quite a natural connection between my work and the Bible. God never treats surface causes, He digs deep to address the festering root. He would like us to identify those festering roots and treat them the right way, but when He sees us struggling to identify what we need to fix, He teaches us as any good parent would.

There is no way I would have learned humility or empathy because, for one, I didn't know I had pride and neither did I know I was apathetic, so how on earth was I going to fix it if I didn't know I had a problem. I was just continuing to live my life not realising that if I didn't work on these festering roots, there will be a situation, and I can guarantee that there will be, that my unprocessed festering roots would sabotage. Joseph needed the pit and prison to watch his dreams come to fruition but without pride and un-forgiveness.

Joseph needed the cupbearer to forget him so that Pharaoh could see God's hand and raise Joseph as the leader of Egypt. Joseph needed the journey to finally be able to come to terms with forgiving his brothers while he was in a position as leader of Egypt. It would have been so much easier for Joseph to have been revengeful because he could, he had the power. No one was going to fault him for imprisoning or even killing his brothers, but if God hadn't dealt with un-forgiveness that could have been brewing and would have possibly made Joseph either imprison or kill his brothers then the twelve tribes of Israel would have been wiped out.

God couldn't let unprocessed feelings or the festering root destroy the destiny He had orchestrated for Joseph.

I look at Joseph's life and I think I may be closer to his emotional state.

We've been hurt by someone closest to us, people whom we thought we could trust but they left us alone to try to scramble out of the pit they had left us in. When that failed, we were left in a situation that looked like there was finally some respite. Just when we think the tide has turned, we're drowning again and we didn't even see the flood coming. We were trying to do the right thing and we're swimming harder than ever, but somehow we're drowning now. More high tides batter us and leave us choking and gasping in the prison before the glimmer of hope we saw actually shows us the way out. The trials are needed because when we're entrusted with a greater responsibility, we need to make sure we're ready for it.

I had learned the key to winning a spiritual battle. There was still a problem I faced. I didn't understand what trusting God truly meant. I had just scratched the surface of my journey. I always believed that I was a Christian and knew the ways of the Lord, but I didn't realise what I didn't know. I slowly unearthed the absolute ignorance and sometimes, arrogance I had regarding my walk with the Lord. I thought I knew what it meant to walk in faith and I believed firmly that I was a terrible Christian. I had done everything wrong that I possibly could have in the eyes of God.

I kept hearing at church about how when someone was saved, they constantly are flooded with elated feelings of heaven and the guarantee of getting there. I knew I was saved, but I wondered if heaven was a guarantee for me. Let's face the reality, I had been a 'good Christian' today, but yesterday, I had lived a less than Christian life. I had spent a few lonely hours thinking about my past and the simpler days when I wasn't saved and wishing I was back there… but wasn't that supposed to be sin in itself? Maybe I wasn't saved? How could a saved Christian reminisce about spending time with friends who were not Christian? Should a Christian really feel lonely? Wasn't I supposed to have God and just be happy? I was happy one day, but that feeling didn't really carry forward every day. I was constantly haunted by the ghosts of my past. It took a few low troughs to understand that my emotions were not just 'a sad feeling'. I was struggling day to day. On the best of days, I could manage to get by without too many panic attacks. On the worst days, I'd get up from the bed, set foot on the floor and immediately feel the monster's embrace. I was battling depression and didn't realise it.

I would sob uncontrollably in the bathroom so that no one would hear me and I would wish that I could just disappear. At that stage, it didn't matter who was around me, because I couldn't handle myself, how could I have the energy to think about someone else? I believed that chain smoking was the next best option to ease the pain away. I tried so hard to get God to love me. I was desperate for Him to love me. I wanted for God to look at me and smile and say those words that He spoke about Job, "That's a righteous person." I had to face the reality that God was never really going to be pleased with me. I had read the Bible; I had meditated on the word. I went to church, I prayed, I thought I did everything I needed to make God feel proud that He created me, and yet somehow I didn't feel that God really loved me. I struggled to feel His acceptance. He was clearly too holy to really be associated with a person like me.

I couldn't see the fundamental theory I had missed. I refused to seek the truth and understand what the Bible really told me about God's love. I chose to fight the battle myself and refused to look at the reality of the true potential of my greatest strength. I refused to use His strength because I believed that I had a plan. I assumed that I knew how to win the battle. I was so wrong that it nearly cost me my own life and cost my children their mother and my parents, their daughter. I figured that I was saved and should be winning all my battles because I assumed that my salvation was automatic battle armour. I fought my battles without actually letting the Bible soak into me. Every day I faced the monster living in my mind, I would crawl back mentally bruised and nearly completely defeated and I could not understand why life was so hard. It genuinely looked like I was the only one who was struggling to survive every waking moment. The battle within myself saw me sitting before doctors lying to convince them that my self inflicted wounds were results of my clumsiness.

Each scar took longer to heal emotionally and finally I decided that I was too imperfect to win this battle, but I still continued to read the Bible, because, at this point, I had firmly disassociated myself with everyone, whether it was the church or outside. I faced several more battles before I came across Hosea 4:6, *"My people are destroyed from lack of knowledge"* and I wondered what this knowledge that I clearly was lacking actually looked like! It took more struggles and battles and near deaths before I realised that I truly was lacking the knowledge of God's love. In the absolute fear of putting money or my career or anything else on the throne of my heart, I had unwittingly put myself on the throne, assuming that I knew the Bible and God enough to fight these battles.

I had refused to ask the author of the Bible to help me with ordering my steps and the wisdom to see the reason behind the struggles. I had refused to put God on the throne to seek His wisdom and understand the lessons that God was trying to teach me. I automatically assumed that I was not good enough to seek His wisdom because He wouldn't care about someone like me. I had not really sought His wisdom in the Bible that I was constantly reading. I couldn't see the truth that was staring me in the face in one of Jesus' parables. I was reading through Luke chapter 15:4 *"Suppose one of you has a hundred sheep and loses one of them. Doesn't he leave the ninety-nine in the open country and go after the lost sheep until he finds it? ⁵ And when he finds it, he joyfully puts it on his shoulders, ⁶ and goes home."* I thought I knew that verse extremely well. I was brought up with the image of Jesus holding a lamb on His shoulder and speaking parables about the lost sheep, the lost coin, and the lost son. All the three parables had the same theme. When the lost son was found, the father was overjoyed, when the lost coin was found, the woman was overjoyed and when the sheep was found, the shepherd was overjoyed. Something in that chapter made me read it again. It was almost as if a bright light flowed through my darkened heart. Verse 4 read, *"Doesn't he leave the ninety-nine in the open country and* **go after the lost sheep until he finds it?"**

He goes after the sheep… He, the shepherd symbolising God, **goes after the sheep**, and that sheep was clearly going in a direction opposite to what God wanted for it. It meant that God will follow His children **in the wrong direction** until He catches up to them… meaning, He never gives up on anyone, wasn't that the whole purpose of Jesus? I was blown away by a rush of God's love. It was amazing. The quintessential verse about God's love is found in John 3:16, *"For God so loved the world that he gave his one and only Son, that whoever believes in him shall not perish but have eternal life."* So why did it take me so long to see what was blatantly staring me in the face? I knew God loved everyone, and that included me as well. Sitting in my new found revelation from an old verse, I wondered why I was so amazed by something I had read before. I understood that God goes after whom He loves because of another verse in 1 John 4:8, *"Whoever does not love does not know God, because God is love."* It wasn't just that God had love toward us, it was because **He is Love**.

No wonder I struggled to understand God, the first half of that verse told me that *if I don't love, I didn't know God*. I thought that verse only spoke about loving others, but looking deeper at it, *how can I love others if I didn't love myself?*

That was precisely the lack of knowledge the Bible was talking about, I didn't know enough about God and His love. I didn't understand the depth of the words that God loved me first. He knew me and the defects that came with who I was and He still loved me because **He IS Love**. He is the same God of the Old and New Testament who absolutely loves mankind, to the point that He was willing to die for us.

God can't love me tomorrow anymore than He does today.

I had to really come to terms with the reality of God's love, and I firmly believe that if I didn't go through what I did, I never would have had to face the reality of what I didn't know. I thought I knew what God's love meant, but if it weren't for the reality that led me to doubt His love, I began to understand what God's love actually meant. I realised that God intended for me to love myself first. He wanted me to see myself the way He saw me. God didn't see me as a weak Christian, struggling every day to stay afloat as the monster tried every day to defeat me. God saw me as perfect and beautiful and as someone whom He had died for, and would do it again if I was the only person on the earth.

He didn't see me as a failure in life, but He saw me as His perfect creation whom He loved beyond life.

He just needed one thing from me, the one thing that set the Old Testament warriors apart... persistence.

Going back to the story of Elijah where he sent his servant *seven* times to see if there was a rain cloud. The number seven, as we've seen before holds great significance biblically and depicts completion, however, I believe that it also signifies persistence. Every time the servant was sent back, it showed Elijah's persistence. The stories of persistence continue throughout the Bible - 2 Kings Chapter 5 talks about Naaman the valiant warrior, who was also a leper.

Elisha, who was the Prophet Elijah's successor stepped in after a bit of drama with the king of Israel and told Naaman to dip himself *seven* times in the river Jordan. Naaman was not happy with the fact that Elisha didn't take the effort to lay hands on him and heal him, but instead asked him to do something so ridiculous in an extremely un-fascinating river. It took him some convincing, but he eventually obeyed Elisha's instructions and he was healed. There's the number seven again to signify completion, but I think this story signified the most important thing for me - healing doesn't come in the most obvious form.

God never works in the obvious. He uses the most unsuspecting ways. No one expected the Saviour of the world to be born in the manger. No one expected Moses to use a stick. No one expected Joshua and Jehoshaphat to use praise to defeat an army. God didn't care that Gideon was hiding when He called him a warrior - He understands the human weaknesses.

God chose to die to reveal resurrection. I had to be ok with some things dying in my life before I could see what He was raising up. It might look like the perfect presentation when someone lifts their hands in church and they are healed in the instant when the preacher speaks healing into their lives. It is never the same manifestation for everyone. What worked for one person is never going to look the same for the next. Jesus taught that in his healings. Let's look at the way Jesus raised people from the dead. Jairus the synagogue leader's daughter had died and Jesus went into the house and despite the people mocking Him, He said the girl was asleep. He raised her up from the dead with *Talitha koum* (Mark 5:21-43). If we look at another death of a person very close to Jesus, that was the family of Mary, Martha, and Lazarus. The gospel of John makes reference to this incident when Lazarus died. Poor Lazarus had to stay dead so Jesus could showcase the miracle of resurrection.

We must remember the basis of all healing or miracles has a deeper set message for us to take away. Whether it be learning to be grateful like with the ten lepers (Luke 17:11-19), or telling the crippled man at the pool of Bethesda to be healed and not to sin again (John 5:14). It always has a deeper lesson and coming to terms with that revelation is what makes the miracle sink deeper.

If I go back to the story of Lazarus, when Jesus heard that he was sick, He declared that this was to showcase God's glory. He went on to not just wait for Lazarus to actually die, but He then told them plainly, *"Lazarus is dead, and for your sake, I am glad I was not there, so that you may believe,"* (John 11).

I can't imagine how distraught Lazarus' sisters would have felt. They had sent word to Jesus that Lazarus was sick and expected Him to drop everything and come rushing back, but He waited for the perfect timing. He was only after one thing, and He spells it out in John 11 verse 4, *"This sickness will not end in death. No, it is for God's glory so that God's Son may be glorified through it."* He knew what the destiny was, and Lazarus' miracle had to take on this form to bring glory to God. Jesus could have stopped Lazarus from dying, but He allowed for it and then Jesus wept (John 11:35). I think that Jesus wept because Lazarus' death was symbolic of His own because the Gospel of John shows this as the last of Jesus' miracles before He is crucified.

Sometimes, the current despair is a precedent for greater glory.

Raising Lazarus symbolised Jesus' own resurrection, but His death was coming first. It was a brutal death, but the end was going to bring glory to God. When we're able to discern the path for God's glory and the fact that it's never going to look the same for everyone, then this is the exact point that we recognise the battle strategy.

God won't always say a yes, but sometimes He will say a no so that He can give you so much grace that you end up achieving something that you could never have thought was inside you. He'll use His no to lead you to unleash a potential even you didn't know you had.

Reading the details in parallel from the Gospels showed me how deliberate Jesus was in His every action. Every single step that He took was to show the usual angst that a Christian would face.

Faith takes the most unusual form when you least expect it and I believe that is exactly why the author of Hebrews wrote in chapter 11 verse 1, *"Now faith is the substance of things hoped for, the evidence of things not seen."* (KJV) The evidence of faith never looks the same. Just because someone else received their miracle through one path, doesn't automatically mean I will receive my healing through the same medium. I just need to become the warrior that God intended me to be, and warriors never give up. I had to understand the revelation of this before I could move any further in my life.

CHAPTER 11

JESUS UNDERSTOOD

D on't put your faith in human beings - you'll be disappointed every time! People's emotional state can make them move very rapidly from *Hosanna* one day *to Crucify Him* the next.

I'd like to believe that God teaches humility because His word shows us that all glory needs to go to Him. John 14:15 says, *"If you love me, keep my commands."* I believe that refers to not just the Ten Commandments that God gave Moses in Exodus 20, but it also includes the two new commandments that Jesus spoke in Matthew 22:36-40, *"'Love the Lord your God with all your heart and with all your soul and with all your mind.' This is the first and greatest commandment. And the second is: 'Love your neighbour as yourself.' All the Law and the Prophets hang on these two commandments."*

Jesus was extremely clear in saying that His new commands didn't mean that the ones from the Old Testament should be ignored, but He says that the new commandments encompass everything. Jesus was pretty clear in saying that we need to love others like ourselves. How on earth can we speak positively about someone else, with true genuine feelings, if we hate everything about ourselves? I could not, with a clear conscience, say that I was truly happy for someone when I was stewing in the bitterness of myself.

Jesus wanted me to first seek help and guidance to sort out my internalised feelings. He drew a perfect connection to help me with my mental state. I believe that He is concerned about the mental state of His children. He gave us the principles in the form of the very first commandment. I believe that He had to spell it out in the New Testament for us because it didn't seem to click for mankind. God, in His infinite wisdom, knew that the greatest territory for the enemy was to control the mind. He knew that if we loved God, we would be able to see ourselves in a different light and then, and only then could we love and or allow ourselves to be loved.

How often had I pushed myself away from everyone because I didn't feel like I deserved to be loved because I refused to see myself how Jesus saw me? I didn't understand the basic formula God had laid out, because I didn't think God worked like that. I didn't think God knew about mental health or even cared, but as I soaked up His word, I discovered that mental stability was a priority on God's mind. I realised this was why He kept reminding us of His love and grace. This is why I never understood why people who were genuinely positive almost always told me, "God is good, you have to taste His love to know that." I began to understand that they had figured out the formula, maybe through some trying situations, but they knew that God was good.

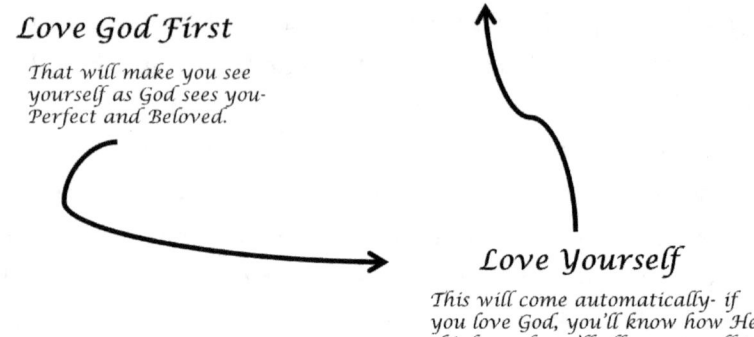

Love Others
This will become genuine because you are filled with genuine love.

Love God First
That will make you see yourself as God sees you- Perfect and Beloved.

Love Yourself
This will come automatically- if you love God, you'll know how He thinks and you'll allow yourself to be loved.

It was so simple to understand the love of God now. When I love God, I fall in love with Him and there was no way I'd ever be able to fall out of love with Him because for the first time I've experienced the purest form of love. He chases us to make sure that He doesn't lose sight of us. It is in some of my lowest points that I discovered some of God's greatest strengths. It is the realisation that it's not our ability that makes a difference in the way we see ourselves, but it is the confidence in how God sees us. It is the childlike faith that He talked about in Matthew 18:2-4 that makes the difference. How was I going to make it through my struggles if I don't humble myself enough to just trust God? I needed to do a complete cleaning of my mental processes; I needed to redirect my faith. It was in the darkest points that I realised that I just could not afford to not have faith in God's love. I began to understand for myself everything that the mighty men of the Bible had struggled through, and yet somehow kept their faith strong in God. They had sought God and found His love so powerful that they could declare that God is good.

Circumstances do not determine God's goodness.

All the songs that I heard and worshipped along with began making sense now. I understood what actually made the writers write these songs and where their heart truly was. I discovered that they had *tasted the Lord*. King David wrote in Psalm 34:8 *"Taste and see that the Lord is good; blessed is the one who takes refuge in him."* This was at the same point where he pretended to be insane and ran away into the cave at Adullam (1 Samuel 21). His emotions fluctuated between Psalm 56 and 34 during this trying time, but he could still say, the Lord is good.

Looking at Jesus' life, He was acutely aware of depression and stayed true to His destiny despite the opposition around. He unashamedly told his disciples, *"My soul is overwhelmed with sorrow to the point of death. Stay here and keep watch with me."* (Matthew 26:36-46). He knew what was coming, and He struggled with it as a man. The prophet Isaiah had already said about Him in Isaiah 53:3, *"He was despised and rejected by mankind, a man of suffering, and familiar with pain…"* Jesus taught us that depression is not something that is our choice, but it is our choice how to react or deal with it. He also taught that depression is not sin, because Hebrews 4:15 says, *"For we do not have a high priest who is unable to empathize with our weaknesses, but we have one who has been tempted in every way, just as we are—yet he did not sin."*

Jesus showed me that it was important to keep the focus on the destiny ahead and not the circumstances around.

David spoke prophetically in Psalm 22 verse 7 and 8, *"All those who see me ridicule me. They shoot out the lip. They shake their heads saying, 'He trusted in the Lord. Let Him rescue him. Let Him deliver him since He delights in him'."*

The story of the cross describes in detail what the people around said to the Messiah as He was dying. Let's go to what actually happened, as recorded again in the Gospel of Matthew, chapter 27 verses 39-43, *[39] "Those who passed by hurled insults at him, shaking their heads[40] and saying, 'You who are going to destroy the temple and build it in three days, save yourself! Come down from the cross, if you are the Son of God!' [41] In the same way the chief priests, the teachers of the law and the elders mocked him. [42] 'He saved others,' they said, 'but he can't save himself! He's the king of Israel! Let him come down now from the cross, and we will believe in him. [43] He trusts in God. Let God rescue him now if he wants him, for he said, 'I am the Son of God'.'"*

Jesus drew attention to Psalm 22 when He hung on the cross. He drew attention to His mental state, which was hanging by a thread at this point. He was perfect, sinless and yet, He was in a situation as a man, having been flogged, spat on and subjected to the worst insults to the point where He was hung naked on the cross. The situation drove Him in Matthew 27:46 to holler with probably the hoarsest voice to heaven, *"Eli, Eli, lema sabachthani?" (Which means "My God, my God, why have you forsaken me?")*. He was on the cross with absolute agony and all He could think about was the loneliness that was engulfing Him. Jesus felt exactly as I did and He believed that in the time of His greatest agony, God had forsaken Him too. He felt deserted at the point when He needed God the most. He needed someone beside Him and at that point - when no one could do anything, He looked to heaven. He understood the struggle of the mind and He experienced some of the worst struggles emotionally. The prophet Isaiah prophesied that He would be a man of sorrow and acquainted with grief (Isaiah 53:3 KJV). When He prayed in the garden of Gethsemane in Matthew 26, He was in absolute anguish and asked God to remove this sorrow from His life. Though He was dealing with grief and torment, He resigned His walk to His Father and accepted that even if this agony could not be removed from Him, He trusted God (verse 39).

He trusted God's love and He knew that sometimes there are some things that need to be lost in order to gain greater glory.

God is in charge of my destiny, but free will makes me in charge of making those decisions to get me to my destiny.

I could believe every one of those powerful verses for others, but I couldn't for myself. I didn't think I was worthy of God. I can firmly say that, unless I chose to really and fervently get to know Him, I would never be able to see His every guidance as one full of love.

Looking back at my life, I don't think I've understood God's love as much as I do now. I was first saved at the age of sixteen, and it's taken me eighteen years since then to reach the point I'm at today, to fully understand what my salvation meant. For eighteen years I've looked at Christianity as the hardest religion. My completely flawed perception of *being saved* was that it was full of rules and laws and some of them were impossible to follow in the modern day and it was overwhelming to be a Christian. I had felt restrained and it was absolutely an uphill task because, in my mind, I lived in a catch- 22 situation. My salvation was governed by man. I was a *born-again saved Christian* but I was so overwhelmed with Christianity that I no longer wanted to be a Christian, but I couldn't get out of Christianity because God knew I didn't want to be a Christian and that surely destined me to hell. I had felt I was restrained by my faith and I hated every bit of it.

Fast forward all these years and struggling with decisions to hold on to a faith that I didn't really want anymore and I realised that it didn't have to be so hard. Looking back, God tried to show me that I was looking at Christianity all wrong because I was so ignorant to His word, and yes, that meant, I was perishing because of my lack of knowledge. It took some extremely dark seasons before I could see that all my life I had never really known God or loved Him. The clichéd sentence, but I knew about Him and thought I loved Him but I still had not come to terms with what that actually meant. It took me to a season of not feeling loved even by God and feeling betrayed by Him before I understood the gravity of my ignorance. I realised that loving God, meant that I followed His word and did everything I could to please Him without feeling like I was forced to. I'm not saying that once I had that revelation I was the epitome of perfection and didn't sin at all, but it simply meant that no matter what happened, I was certain that He loved me because my foundation was planted in His love. Jesus continued to spell it out in Luke 6 and Matthew 7 where He speaks, in slightly varying verses, of judging others, loving our enemies, bearing good fruit, false prophets and then about building the house on the solid rock.

The key here, I think, is in Matthew 7:25 and Luke 6:48 which describes the house built on a rock but that did not guarantee the house would not face the buffeting waves and the gales. It just meant that the house would be lashed out at, but would still stand strong. Jesus goes on to explain that anyone who doesn't put His words into practice was like the house that was certain to fall and crash. No wonder I thought Christianity was a struggle each time the winds blew. I had to really re-look at scripture to understand what was expected of me. Jesus wanted me to look at my relationship with Him as one where love dictates my every action.

His love was the path that ordered my steps everyday.

Looking at a simple example, if a husband and wife were completely in love with each other, would either of them stray, knowing the pain it might cause the other? Their love for each other keeps them motivated to do the right thing for the relationship. I think it means exactly the same thing in any relationship. There are ups and downs that come with the territory of every relationship, but in effect, no one who is invested in the relationship would even consider it a burden to do anything for the other person. This holds true for my relationship with God as well. I didn't see giving up some things as a burden anymore, I saw it as what I did out of love and because I wanted to.

The reality still remained that I struggled with my emotions on a constant basis, because the brutal reality is that the enemy was not going to give up trying to defeat me just because I had a new revelation. I had to fight the monster off daily and the battles became fiercer but easier at the same time. I had to face doubts of mammoth proportions of my new found revelation when things went wrong, but it became easier to say and believe that even if God doesn't save me from this situation, it doesn't change the fact that God is still on the throne because I trust His judgement. I understood what Jesus was trying to explain in the New Testament. He had to dumb the Old Testament so that my brain could fathom it all.

I deeply believed that God understood the struggles of mankind, but I was convinced He surely didn't understand the struggles of heartbreak and falling out of love. What could break God's heart? Jeremiah 3:8 answers, *"I gave faithless Israel her certificate of divorce and sent her away…"* My separation from the man I believed was my soul mate was my darkest point, but I began to feel a weight being lifted off. God knew what divorce felt like. The same God who loved Israel, and when I say love, I don't mean the human type shallow love, His love was DEEP and it was unconditional! I can't even begin to fathom His pain when He divorced Israel, and this verse really hit home.

He doesn't choose Israel or us based on what we've achieved or haven't, but Deuteronomy 7:7-8 says, *"The LORD did not set His love on you nor choose you because you were more in number than any other people, for you were the least of all peoples; but because the LORD loves you..."*

There was just something else I had to understand with the battles that God was slowly trying to reveal to me through His word. I was becoming more eager to soak up all the knowledge God had to offer. I knew already that my mind was prime enemy territory and if he could defeat me in the most vulnerable territory, then he had defeated my family too. Innocent people were going to become victims of a bloodbath that the monster had already set in its sights. I had to fight the battle continually harder than before with a new arsenal of weapons.

CHAPTER 12

MIND VS MOUTH

knew that God wanted me to use this powerful weapon in its most raw form. I didn't need to think through it theologically or try to understand it for more than what it truly was intended to be.

In 2 Chronicles chapter 20 the battlefield is described that King Jehoshaphat was in the middle of. He was going to be attacked by a vast army in verse 2 and clearly by what was going on, there was no way he was going to win that battle. He did what he needed to do when his life was clearly in danger and he knew that something more than his army was his only respite. He headed to the temple of God and stood before God and spoke of all the victories he had seen and heard of. He did not immediately focus on the impending doom but instead he focused on the victories and then he told God that he was sure of God's hand that would save him and his army. He didn't stand there alone; he had all his people and their families standing helpless before God. Amazingly, God explained through the prophets there that King Jehoshaphat shouldn't really worry about the battle because that's God's playing field. God was the military genius in battle.

The next few verses amazed me as I pictured the battle. Here was the army of Jehoshaphat in full armour ready for the war and he was telling his people to keep their faith in God, though they had not seen victory yet. All they could see was the enemy closing in on them in droves, yet they held on to the invisible. Jehoshaphat then did what probably will never make sense to the human mind; he began to praise God and sing of God's goodness. How unsettling would that have been to a king who knew that killing the enemy was the only way to see victory? He probably had second thoughts, I know I would have, but there was something in that chapter that showed me that Jehoshaphat knew the key to battlefield victory better than anyone. This was not the kind of praise when you buy a new house; this was an extraordinary praise that was used when you're uncertain of life or death in the next few minutes, and yet somehow you're certain of victory. It takes someone who had an extraordinary relationship with God to be able to put his praise into context, even when there was no guarantee that he would get out of the battle alive. The strategy worked and the Lord gave them the victory.

It was not a random isolated praise party that Jehoshaphat had decided to be a part of. He was part of a praise that showed that he had been through worse times and had come out unscathed. What amazed me was that praise seemed to come naturally to Jehoshaphat, so this was not a new strategy he had discovered.

This was also the foundation of Joshua. We've read about the warrior in Joshua, but we didn't revisit the praise party that Joshua threw in the midst of certain defeat. The city of Jericho loomed before him (Joshua 6). He was facing a monster bigger than him or his army. Joshua, a warrior, quite similar to Jehoshaphat knew that the sure fire way to get victory… was to attack the enemy with physical weapons. It struck me as amazing that Joshua knew his limitations as a warrior and knew that this was more than he could or should be taking on. He simply went to the greatest battle strategy. He understood the power of praise and after he led the loud shout of praise, he watched the mighty walls that were holding back his destiny crumble and fall. It must have been quite a spectacular event for Joshua to watch the first brick tumble down. It might have made them gasp in awe and probably raise the shout of praise even louder. What an awesome moment to get the supernatural victory.

Then there was the book of Daniel where Daniel's friends Shadrach, Meshach, and Abednego were going to be thrown into the fire for believing in God, (Daniel 3).

Here were three young men who were dragged in before the king, and they were probably not led to the king on a bed of flowers. They were probably beaten or pushed or faced some intimidation before being presented to the king. They still were able to stand and face the person who literally held their lives in his power, and tell him respectfully, *[17] "'If we are thrown into the blazing furnace, the God we serve is able to deliver us from it, and he will deliver us from Your Majesty's hand. [18] But even if he does not, we want you to know, Your Majesty that we will not serve your gods or worship the image of gold you have set up.'"*

The first part in Daniel 3 verse 17 would be hard enough to mouth, let alone form such eloquent words but verse 18 pushed me into the minds of these men. They were filled with faith to the brim that God was able to save them, and even if God didn't save them, they would still worship Him. Questions began to arise about did they really have faith when they weren't sure if God was going to save them. Did they really have faith when they didn't trust God's saving hand?

Faith doesn't always change your situation. Faith is keeping my eyes on the Creator and not on the situation.
Faith is not proved by a change in circumstances.

Faith is not faith only when God proves He's God, but faith is even when He doesn't prove He is God. Faith shouldn't exist only when I get what I want, but also when I don't. Faith is not only in the God who saves, but it is faith in God even when He doesn't. I'm sure they would have liked God to rain fire on the wicked king Nebuchadnezzar to prove He is Almighty God. It probably was what they wanted, but not what they got. They were met with a king whose anger against them grew so much that he heated the furnace seven times more than usual and had the three men bound (Daniel 3:19-23). The flames were so hot that the soldiers who threw the men in ended up getting burnt. Can you imagine the terror of the three bound men as they fell into the scorching fire? Imagine watching the soldiers being burned alive and the smell of burnt flesh, and knowing that they were next. It was not long before the very king who ordered them to be thrown in the furnace and was seated there waiting to watch them burn in that fire, jumped up when he saw something extraordinary. He yelled out in amazement, [24] *"'Weren't there three men that we tied up and threw into the fire?* [25] *Look! I see four men walking around in the fire, unbound and unharmed, and the fourth looks like a son of the gods.'"*

    A few millennia later as we read this story, we're so grateful for God's saving grace on the lives of those three men, but what if it was me headed to the furnace? How grateful would I have been in the face of certain death, and a cruel one at that? The test was in verse 27 of Daniel chapter 3, when they stepped out without the smell of smoke on them. Thank God for letting Shadrach, Meshach, and Abednego face the fire. I would never have known what true faith meant otherwise. They praised God for what they couldn't see.

    If this was a seemingly Old Testament trend, then there was another fascinating story in the New Testament to reiterate this. Acts 16 made a good read to illustrate the power of praise. Here were Paul and Silas dragged to prison because they had cast a demon out of a lady. Before we go to the prison, let's look at this strange attack by the enemy. He knew what to do to get under Paul's skin. It wasn't anything that I possibly would have readily discerned because all that the lady in Acts 16 verse 17 said was, *"These men are servants of the Most High God, who are telling you the way to be saved."* I didn't see anything wrong with that, she was after all stating in the truth. This verse shows us that the enemy knows all too well how to use his strategic weapons. Paul, somehow discerned that she was possessed and cast the demons out of her. To this day, I still don't know how he discerned that, but it turned out to be true. She was set free from the demon that possessed her, but with her freedom came shackles for the men who brought her that freedom. Paul and Silas would end up in prison and that should have been the end of the gospel and all the signs and wonders. That's almost what happened. Here are Paul and Silas, who were dragged before the magistrates who ordered more humiliation to be hailed down by stripping them and having them beaten with rods. Then they were thrown into prison, no doubt mocked by the prisoners and prison guards. The prison guard then proceeded to shackle their feet to make sure that they couldn't escape.

The jail cell saw the battered, bruised, and bloodied faces and bodies of Paul and Silas. The jail cell smelled of fresh and clotted blood from these two men. The jail cell also heard something starting to overpower the sounds of agony filled moans and groans... the soft singing rising above the pain coming from the cell of Paul and Silas. The other prisoners listened to them sing and then came the earth-shattering earthquake. The prison doors flew open and the shackles holding Paul and Silas fell loose. The prison guard was so shaken in the darkness to the extent that he nearly killed himself with his own sword. He couldn't imagine the repercussions he would face from the magistrates because he was sure the prisoners, whom he was asked to be extra watchful over, would have fled the jail cell. Not Paul and

Silas, there was something in them that didn't let them ignore the need to save one more soul at the cost of their own. They called out to the jailer and stopped him from killing himself. The story reiterates the simple battle strategy that God has been teaching right from the Old Testament... praise breaks chains. Right then I had a choice, I could either let my chains break me or my praise break those chains.

I'm not saying that praising in the prison is an easy decision by a long stretch. I am speaking for myself here. I know how I would have reacted if it was me bound before the king waiting for my fate in the fire, or in the prison cell. It would have been nothing close to the way these men reacted. The challenge I had before me was to fall on my knees and learn *how* to praise my chains away. I felt a wild rush over me as my brain raced back to the day I had heard the song that kept ringing in my ears, *"... praise His name... You can praise the hurt away, if you'll just praise His Name."* I understood. This was the piece of the jigsaw that I had been missing. I understood that God was trying to teach me something, not out of rage or infuriation or to teach me a lesson, but in His infinite love to refine me. He had just taught me the greatest battle strategy that I would never have been able to see on my own. I needed my own fire and furnace, my own jail cell, my own Jericho and my own Goliath to tell my story. I would have never had the opportunity to have my greatest trial help someone else out of theirs. This became my focus now. Praising God did not remove the pain itself, but it removed the impact of the pain on my life because my focus was on God and not the pain. I stopped asking *why me.*

I understood the familiar theme I needed to tackle. The monster was bigger than anyone could imagine. I needed to know that I could never defeat the monster by myself and even to try was useless. I had to depend on someone greater than myself, because how else could the glory go to Him? If I won the battle myself then the furnace or prison cell wouldn't have the same impact as it would with God's strength. The furnace would never have been able to tell the compelling story without the fourth man. I needed to praise the chains away, and this was what the enemy was keeping me from focusing on.

The Bible explicitly talks about the warfare not being of this world but a spiritual one with the enemy and the weapons we use are not of this world either. I believe it was the weapons of praise that the Bible speaks about in 2 Corinthians 10:4. I began to realise that praise is not simply chanting the words, "Praise you Jesus" a thousand times while my mind was still on the struggles ahead. It is the greatest act of worship to fulfil why we as humans were created for as seen in Isaiah 43:7, *"Everyone who is called by my name, whom I created for my glory, whom I formed and made."* The enemy is not going to stand by and allow us to worship because that was his role initially. Going back to a translation of the book of Ezekiel, it shows me that Lucifer or Satan was created to worship God and when pride set into Satan, God enforced judgement, something He has never had to do until then. The New King James Version (NKJV) shows Satan created as a supreme angel and maybe a chief musician because God writes *"…The workmanship of your timbrels and pipes was prepared for you on the day you were created,"* (Ezekiel 28:31 NKJV). The enemy is not going to allow mankind to fulfil what was his role, and he is well aware of his power. God sees us as able to fill that void of worship and praise in heaven and that's why He's said to inhabit the praise of His people in Psalm 22:3 (NKJV). The enemy knows fully well what praise and worship can do, it can bring heaven to earth and he will do anything to stop us from having the power that he was denied.

If I were to look at 1 Samuel 16:23, I see the story of Saul being oppressed by an evil spirit and David, who was known for singing praise unto God, would worship God and the evil spirit would leave Saul. The enemy knows the power of praise. He knows that praise can break chains and praise can help us see ourselves in the same light that God sees us. That is a disaster for the enemy. He knows that once we see ourselves through God's eyes, we are not going to see anything but the destiny that we were called to fulfil. We are going to be propelled a hundred percent in the direction of our calling, which is to use our talents and gifts to serve others. We are taught endlessly about worship in a corporate setting, but worship is not just the twenty or thirty minutes we are attuned to at the start of a Sunday morning service. Worship is obedience to God. It is thanking Him, not for what He has done, but praising Him for who He is. The crux of praise is found in Colossians 3:17, *"And whatever you do, whether in word or deed, do it all in the name of the Lord Jesus, giving thanks to God the Father through him."* And in 1 Thessalonians 5:16-18, *[16] "Rejoice always, [17] pray continually, [18] give thanks in all circumstances; for this is God's will for you in Christ Jesus."*

Praise is not limited to one day a week; it is in *everything* we do. It was one of the greatest challenges I've had, to look beyond the situation and keep my eyes on the Maker.

My level of praise went hand in hand with my level of forgiveness. Like praise, forgiveness was a choice I had to make. I had to choose forgiveness because there was no greater injustice that I could inflict on myself by replaying everything over and over to myself. If I chose to hold on to the pain caused that would only lead me to a place where I stopped functioning as to what I knew I was capable of.

Unforgiveness cripples the power of praise.

Modern day psychology has researched time and time again the effects of unforgiveness on the human brain and body (Toussaint, Shields, Dorn, & Slavich, 2014). The researchers said that they thought forgiveness would knock something off the relationship between stress and psychological distress, but they didn't expect it to zero it out.

Further studies showed that forgiveness was directly linked to better mental health (Toussaint, Shields, & Slavich, 2016). There are more extensive research studies done on the link between forgiveness and better mental health, and the Bible, for me personally, was far ahead of its times in showcasing forgiveness as part of God's nature. Psalm 103:8-12 reads, *"The LORD is merciful and gracious, slow to anger and abounding in steadfast love. He will not always chide, nor will he keep his anger forever. He does not deal with us according to our sins, nor repay us according to our iniquities. For as high as the heavens are above the earth, so great is his steadfast love toward those who fear him; as far as the east is from the west, so far does he remove our transgressions from us."*

The Bible also says that we ought to try and emulate Jesus who was God in every way. [5] *"In your relationships with one another, have the same mindset as Christ Jesus:* [6] *Who, being in very nature God, did not consider equality with God something to be used to his own advantage,"* (Philippians 2:5-6). And goes on to say, *"Whoever claims to live in him must live as Jesus did,"* (1 John 2:6). Forgiveness is in the very nature of God, even upon the cross. He was forever thinking about others. I think God doesn't look at if we've achieved a certain standard of excellence, instead He only cares about the effort we put into the race.

God never intended for me to enter each day as a victim. That was never the purpose of Him creating me. The Bible is rife with examples where strong men of faith have not given up or given in to the situation. The greatest example is Apostle Paul who spoke of his struggles not to draw pity towards himself, but to build up the faith of others. The Apostle Paul was not ashamed of his scars or his experiences. He was genuine about his struggles with the sole intention of using his scars as a story to strengthen others.

Strength comes from the scars that we unashamedly display.

Reading the book of Philippians, I could see what the Apostle Paul's scars and shackles meant to him. I am able to relate to his journey through Malta where God had told him that he would preach at Rome, but he didn't preach at Rome as he had intended. He was not as privileged as most preachers to preach from a pulpit, he was actually given shackles. He spoke about what happened to him (Philippians 1:12), and I believe he was referring to probably what was the worst humiliation for a once respected leader.

I couldn't imagine walking down the streets of such an extravagant city like Rome, being shackled and dragged down the streets and beaten by the guards. Funnily, Apostle Paul did not look at his chains as chains. He saw them as trophies. He did preach down the streets of Rome... in chains, but to him, they were a gateway into someone else's chains. He never saw himself there as being chained and he rejoiced in verse 18. He saw his chains as a gateway for his story to bring strength to others. He knew that there were many others who were filled with fear because they were struggling with the same chains. He unashamedly, and I'll go as far as to say proudly, showed off his chains because he knew the chains had value. He wanted everyone going through similar struggles to know that they could shake off the fear and loneliness and the feeling that they were in this battle alone because here was someone who had found purpose in his chains.

Paul found purpose in his chains.

He refused to let his chains make him a prisoner. He was never going to be a victim to his chains. He was going to use everything that was handed to him to reach his destiny… the pulpit or chains.

God showed me something through my journey of absolute horror and despair, that there was absolutely no point in fighting the battles myself. I was never going to win. How many people was I going to convince? For every one person I convinced, five more would crop up who didn't believe me. Was this even worth my energy? Was this the reason I was put on earth… to convince people about my worth? I had to leave the battle to the Lord, because all the verses I had grown up with began to sink in and were now real. I began to understand why the Lord said in 2 Chronicles 20:15, *"Do not be afraid or discouraged because of this vast army. For the battle is not yours, but God's."*

Apostle Paul, despite all the struggles on earth, realised this intrinsically and that's why he wrote in 2 Corinthians 10:4, *"The weapons we fight with are not the weapons of the world."* He also spoke of the armour we need for battle in Ephesians 6:10-17, none of it was a polished sword or spear, but it was faith and righteousness and the like. He was in chains as he wrote this and yet, he realised that his destiny was impeded by something that physical artillery could not war against.

The key was in what Apostle Paul chose to do in chains. He chose, he made a conscious decision to find a purpose in his pain and he did it proudly.

He chose to see someone else's pain through his chains.

CHAPTER 13

HOW DID I MISS THE RED FLAGS?

F or the sake of this chapter, I'm going to refer to the abuser as male and the abused as female, for no other reason except that it was my experience. I'm going to look at a highly contentious topic because the church would like to believe that domestic violence or intimate partner abuse doesn't happen within the church setting, after all, Christians don't do that! I remember every time a sermon was preached about marriage, the quintessential verse that needed to be quoted was *wives, submit to your husbands*. It would make my stomach turn and I was torn between what that meant, and my intuition told me that it did not mean the way it was construed. More often than not, it was preached by men from the pulpit and there would be accompanying funny stories about women who didn't like submission.

Why do the verses in Ephesians 5:22-24 make every modern day woman's skin crawl? It is probably the verse that an abuser feeds on and if you've been in any sort of relationship with an abusive Christian, you have heard it at some stage of your abuse. [22] "*Wives, submit yourselves to your own husbands as you do to the Lord.* ²³ *For the husband is the head of the wife as Christ is the head of the church, his body, of which he is the Savior.* ²⁴ *Now as the church submits to Christ, so also wives should submit to their husbands in everything."* I believe this is one of the most misquoted verses and purely used as a trump card by abusers and is always taken out of context. Submission is used unjustly by abusers, and in particular, Christian abusers to bring the Christian woman to her knees. I think the reason I detest that verse is because of the way it was twisted. It was some of the most insensitive sermons, but it wasn't until I had the courage to leave my abuser, which made me think about all the subtle signs I had missed and how many times I had heard him say, "You should submit to me. The Bible says so." I heard that spat at me even after I left him and all I could think of was how foolish I had been. I was so twisted into his net of lies and manipulation that I would constantly berate myself for bringing my own life to ruin. I blamed myself for being rebellious and not submitting to him, but that meant he didn't have to shoulder any of the blame for being abusive. That verse gave him leeway to abuse me into submission.

    Those thoughts have not completely left me and the guilt is unimaginable on some days. It eats away at my mind as I watch myself replay all the horrendous days and wonder if it was really my fault. He always said that *I made him angry* or that *our marriage was fine until I opened my mouth and ruined it.* Words I had come to accept as part of the territory of marriage, because I didn't know any better. I grew up in a culture and society where men speaking to women in a demeaning manner was the norm, and it was appreciated by the rest of the society. A man controlling everything about his wife was considered truly male and was deemed to have good leadership qualities.

    Growing up in India taught me that a woman is never given the chance to stand up to any man, and right from a young age, she's taught that submission to men is mandatory. She is not given the freedom to choose anything, and it must be chosen for her… by the men in her life who seek advice from other men. Education was decided for her, and her mother plays a non-existent decision-making role in her life as well, because the general consensus was that women are ignorant and need a man to survive in a male dominated society.

Having lived in that controlling culture, I didn't realise or know any different. I grew up completely blind to my strengths because the only strengths I knew were told to me by the male figures in my life. Growing up in an oppressive culture such as India doesn't leave a woman much to look forward to. Her life cycle revolved around her father, brothers, uncles or other male relatives, her husband and then her son and finally her son in law.

I recall vividly stories about a close male relative who would visit my mother's family as she was growing up and apparently this man would grab the girls in the family, quite roughly, either pinching their noses or kicking them on their backsides. They'd protest, but feebly, because this man was a very close relative to their father which automatically meant, their protests were useless. That relative would continue to visit our house and the same behaviour started with me when I was a teenager. Funnily, even my father didn't stop him and it was then I realised that I was never going to be protected, not even in my own family. The only advice I heard was, "Just stay away from him if you don't like it." Looking back, now I understand where that advice came from, but as a teenage girl, I detested it because it meant that the relative was never going to be held accountable for doing something that I was not comfortable with and that gave him permission to continue with no repercussions. I finally had enough after being kicked on the backside or groped for a few years on his weekly visits. I snapped back at him and told him, "The next time you kick me, I will kick you back." And he just looked stunned at me and then my parents and when they thankfully did not side with him, he simply said, "Oh, did you take it seriously? I was only joking. No one has ever spoken to me like this. My goodness, what an attitude you have for such a young girl." All of a sudden, I was branded as the girl who had no respect for her elders. I was labelled as disrespectful and arrogant.

The news spread to every extended family member that everyone should stay away from me and they should keep their children away from me, because who wanted their kids to grow up 'arrogant' like me? I was angry and so hurt that I didn't have a voice to back my side of the story, but my culture did not allow it. Somehow, the men being sexually aggressive didn't stop and it began with relatives, but spiralled to almost every man whom I crossed paths with.

The next relative, with an extremely important role and status within the family, decided that he would try to unexpectedly hug me from behind and try pick me up with the world's most ridiculous excuse saying, "I can tell you how much you weigh without using a weighing scale." First of all, I didn't want to know how much I weighed as a twelve or thirteen year old, secondly, we had a perfectly good weighing scale! I protested first to him and then to my family and I was met with the same response, "You're over thinking it. He doesn't have any wrong intentions. He's always done this with others and only you seem to have a problem with everything." Again, it meant that unfortunately I had to take matters into my own young hands. I ended up kicking him and was met with a unanimous gasp from the whole family. They profusely apologised to him and said, "She's only a young girl and doesn't know what she's doing. Let her be." I was then told off for being disrespectful to him.

I never understood to this day what I did wrong and why my family stopped going to bat for me as I grew up. I remember the first time a man exposed himself to me was a friend of a neighbour when I was about five and I told my parents. My parents were furious with the man and I felt safe, but something changed as I grew up. I couldn't understand why they didn't feel the need to protect me anymore but left me to my own devices. Maybe they thought I could handle it, or maybe it was easier to call it sexual abuse or inappropriate because it was a stranger, it must have been harder to call out relatives on sexual advances.

There was just a small problem with that plan though, I ended up fighting all my battles and defending myself pretty aggressively, and that got me labelled as disrespectful and arrogant. I started seeing more sexual advances as I grew older, and when I say older, I was still less than eighteen years old. Getting groped in the bus so often and having lewd comments and glances thrown toward me and my friends, left us shielding the vulnerable parts of our bodies with our bags or arms.

By no means was I the only one subjected to this behaviour, it continues even today and has probably become worse. It became a norm to expect this behaviour to my daily commute to school and university. Speaking about it to anyone didn't help, because the reply would be, "What were you wearing? Were you covered up or did you invite this attention? No man will touch a girl if she walks quietly with her head bent. Did you behave like a girl?" I had no idea what that last statement was supposed to mean. The fear of being violated and knowing that it was an extremely male-dominated culture meant that it would be a case of victim blaming.

I worked so hard to protect myself that it became second nature. It was near impossible to trust any man, except my father, and then there were the wolves that lay in waiting for a chance where they'd get me or any girl alone. It was a constant minefield to make sure that I didn't get caught out alone, day or evening, making sure I got home before four in the evening. There were terrifying thoughts that invaded my head when a man walked too close or followed me while I walked home from the bus stop. The sigh of relief that I heaved when I was just brushed up against and had not ended up brutally raped or murdered. The fear to retaliate when my friends and I were heckled by large groups of men while we waited for the bus to university, because they had strength in numbers. We didn't want to anger them, because we knew from the papers and the news what happened to girls and women, so we just stood quietly.

The Indian media filled my senses with images of brutally murdered women who were gang raped, and the bloodthirsty wolves began to seek younger victims, until girls as young as one were raped. Then they started feasting on boys, and it reached a stage, where no one was safe. The mob, once it found its victim, was first to attack their dignity and strip them of their clothes. They were tied to trees and beaten, or tied to the back of a car and dragged through streets or have some of the worst atrocities known to man done to them. Fear multiplied within me as more stories infiltrated the media. These stories were happening everyday and I was stuck in the fear that it could happen to me too. I began to understand why women were submissive to men - they were just abused into it. It was not by choice, because women weren't given any. The public humiliation would scare any human, and whether we like to admit it or not, women are gripped by fear every day and the fear grows as the clock ticks past five or six in the evening. I completely understood why women just caved in to the men's authority and didn't even put up a fight, because they knew it was a raw sexual battle in its worst form.

I began to understand why girls at the *marriageable age,* which was around 22 or 23 years were quickly married off. They would be safer in the hands of their own man than to be left to be preyed on by strangers. It explained why girls over that age were considered as a *loose character,* because the mentality was crude enough to decide that if a woman didn't want to be submissive to one man, then she must have several. I understood why a woman didn't have the option to look at her career, because for a woman her husband was all she needed to be focussed on. It was the safe route. It made sense why a woman was almost pawned off to her husband who would be someone who could now take care of her and protect her.

This is fed into a girl's mind right from that *marriageable age* and she's conditioned to learn that her ultimate safe haven is in her husband's house and family. She is expected to leave her own family behind and absorb herself into her husband's family and is almost a slave to their family. This is regardless of family status in society; the expectation is the woman must submit. I was subjected to the same thought process and was constantly bombarded by people telling me, "You must study well, otherwise you won't get married to a good boy" or, "If you go out in public with your friends and laugh so loudly, you think any man will want to marry you?" or, "No man wants his wife to stay out late, so be home early."

Everything revolved around pleasing the future unknown husband and when you've been conditioned to this from a young age, you don't know any different and begin to live your life to please this mystery husband. Considering choosing your own life partner was a topic never discussed and the most stupid reason I recall was, "How can you think of finding a boyfriend? Will your husband be happy if he knew you had a boyfriend?" It was ridiculous as it was infuriating. The idea that a boyfriend could become a husband was an alien concept and was considered too vulgar even to discuss. The term *boyfriend* itself was considered vulgar.

I began to slowly understand that this was the norm and I had to see my future husband as my saviour and someone who would protect me because women really have no power in a man's world. I genuinely had believed that this unknown man would be my saviour and his family would treat me like their own and life would be what it was destined to be. I was blinded by the fact that my husband would protect me from the world that I didn't even consider the possibility of what would happen if I needed to be protected from my husband?

CHAPTER 14

ABUSED INTO SUBMISSION

My parents did everything in a bid to keep me safe and looked around for the perfect match for me. I didn't want marriage at all, but since that was not up for debate, the best option was that a pastor's only son would be the safest bet, which was a general consensus. Here was the epitome of perfection that every parent wanted for their daughters and I was made to feel extremely grateful that he had accepted to marry me and be my *Prince Charming*. I began to hear from everyone as they exclaimed, "You are so lucky that you found such a good man and you don't know how lucky you are that he agreed to marry you, and even his family agreed. You don't know what a great blessing that is."

Having been inured from a young age that I needed a man for my future to be safe and now hearing from people closest to me about how fortunate I was and how finally finding a man was the best thing that had ever happened to me made me automatically and unknowingly accept that I indeed was lucky and extremely fortunate. I was chosen by a pastor's family as their daughter-in-law to their only son.

He was absolutely delightful, there's no denying it. He proclaimed to have never touched alcohol or cigarettes and that was enough to bowl over my parents. He was extremely respectful to the rest of my family and everyone was delighted with him. They would look forward to him visiting and would talk endlessly about him and to him. Innocence, naiveté call it what you please, made them tell him, "She needs to appreciate how lucky she is to have found you. You might be able to keep her attitude in check. She even yelled at the (very important relative) just for kicking her playfully. You'll need to keep her under control." It was the norm for the family of the bride to, for lack of a better word, to talk down the bride to make the groom feel welcome and comfortable. It was probably stupid, in hindsight, but I was not privileged in foresight. He lapped up every bit of information about me, all along feigning laughter, but there was no way I could have known what he planned to do with this information.

Here I was, excited with my *luck* and I accepted everything that was said, including some wild exaggeration that he didn't see as an exaggeration. He knew that I had an option to stop the wedding if I was to have the slightest indication of the reality of who he was, so he handed me rose-tinted frames, so all the red flags just looked like flags. Little did I realise that he was what the stuff of nightmares were made of. I was so blind by the desire to be protected that I was glad that a man had agreed to marry me and be that protector.

Without my rose tinted glasses now, reliving the past is physically revolting. For example, the subtle pushes through the door, the hand holding that was just a little too rough or brushing past me that had unnecessary force so I tipped backward. My husband's smile that followed made me think it was always an accident and that I had nothing to worry about. The lies started following soon and I was always in limbo about the truth.

I wasn't sure if he was really who he was showing himself as. I was just matched up with him all part of the intricate *arranged marriage* and though

I had all these questions, I never actually had a forum to voice them because they seemed like common apprehensions any newlywed would have.

The controlling started so subtly that I didn't even realise it. The first incident of raw aggression I believe was, my husband taking control of my body to satisfy his physical desire. Though the incident itself is too raw to speak about, unexpectedly discovering his secret addiction to porn explained it. I recall vividly speaking about it later to a few relatives, and I heard some of the most obscene advice, "Watching porn is not a big deal. You just need to accept it." And here I was, foolishly expecting that a marriage covenant meant that either spouse doesn't do what the other doesn't like, or at least seek help especially if it was an addiction.

I stayed in the nightmare hoping things would change, but they seemed to escalate, but not too rapidly. My ex-husband was too smart for that. Everything he did made him fly under the radar so everyone around saw me like the crazed lunatic who was angry or upset or struggling to cope while he seemed unfazed by everything. He'd just smile and in the softest voice almost repeat back to them what they had told him about me, "You know her right? She'll get over it. She's just overreacting. She's got quite a bit of an attitude." And this time, they lapped up his theories.

I spent days beating myself up for my life ending up the way it did. I genuinely believed that I was going crazy. I saw myself through his eyes, and since he saw me as a crazy belligerent lunatic, then that was exactly what I saw. If he saw me as worthless, then I mirrored that behaviour. Another simple example was, if he said, "Don't apply for that job, you can never get it," I believed him and I watched my self-worth shrink into non-existence.

He began to isolate me from my friends. He would go into jealous rages if I spoke to any colleague or friends on the phone. But his rage was never a public spectacle. It would always be in the privacy of our room and I had to do everything to show evidence that it was just a work-related phone call.

He made me put the call on speaker so he could hear the other side of the conversation, but the rules were different for him. He would never speak on the phone in my presence but would walk away to another room or to the backyard and tell me, "It's personal and has nothing to do with you. You wouldn't understand the conversation." Statements like that began to feed into my thinking and I started believing that *maybe I really was that stupid.* It's amazing how words will destroy your self-worth, but it's the slowest poison known to man, and you never know you're being poisoned until it's too late. He would randomly follow me to my work place to see if I was at work and then go around telling everyone that I chose to work night shifts because I had affairs all over town. There was no sensible way to prove that I wasn't having affairs, so I'd watch him park by my office and sit there for my whole shift. My brain stopped functioning gradually, and I began to lose interest in everything, including living. I was terrified to speak to anyone, men or women. He didn't really care what he accused me of, as long as he was *one up on me.* He even isolated me from my closest friend by telling my relatives that I had a lesbian relationship with her.

I had reached a point, where he had the pin numbers to my bank cards, my phone, and my email passwords. It all happened so slowly that I had no idea I had given him access to everything myself, all in a bid to prove to him that he was my number one priority. I had no idea that he had been saving all my passwords so he could constantly keep track of what I was doing. If I ever told him I had had enough and wanted to leave him, he would sulk in the presence of my family and when they wanted to know why he was upset, he'd immediately say that I was planning to leave him because I wanted to be with another man. My brain would contort itself trying to figure out this man I had married and all I could see were the flaws in me. Maybe I was doing things that were not right in the scheme of marriage.

Maybe I was putting up a fight for something trivial, maybe I was meant to just *submit*.

I remember the one incident where I wanted to know about his ever elusive bank statements that I was cut so badly with a knife that my sobbing and visibly distraught mother was left mopping the gushing blood. I wasn't sure if I had severed an artery and honestly didn't care because my mind was focused on watching the monster I was married to look at me with such emptiness in his eyes and no reaction that I began to wonder if he was even human. I had let the physical monster's abuse join forces with the one already living in my mind and they were winning together. I looked at the emergency department doctor who asked me the same questions in several different ways trying to ascertain how I had injured myself because I was trying and clearly failing to convince him about the injury. I was partially paralysed by the fear of my abuser who had managed to whisper in my ear, "If they find out, you will end up in jail" and who was now standing by the bedside as the doctor was preparing the wound to be held together by several stitches. I vividly remember the doctor glancing at him when he asked me again about how I was cut, but he gave up on trying to get the truth from me, instead he chose to believe my lies and accepted that *I was trying to catch my dog and fell on a roll of coiled up barbed wire in the garden and had managed to cut myself so perfectly.* I had to call in sick the next day and lied that I had met with an accident, and that lie has stayed with me for about eight years. It makes me retch when I relive that day, so the lie is easier to swallow. The amazing part of it was that he fed on the confusion of that day. He began to spin lies about what actually happened.

A few years later, just having given birth to my second baby, and the stress of living with a monster, I ended up sitting in front of my family doctor being prescribed anti-depressants to help calm me down. Every bit of my wilting mental state was discussed in the presence of the monster I was married to who used every iota of it to his advantage. Soon after that, a similar argument about his bank statements, that had evaded my eyes from the time we were married, led to a forced overdosing of those same antidepressants.

This time, I stood in front of the emergency room nurse who eyed me and the monster who had driven me to the hospital. She asked me, "What happened? How did you overdose?" So, I automatically said, "I accidentally took more than the prescribed dose because I have a new baby and I was distracted." Only I knew why I lied. I had my abuser tell me on the way to the hospital, "If your organisation finds out that you overdosed, then you will lose your job and the police will take you away. You will lose the kids." I knew it was not true because he made me overdose, but in my current mind frame, I really did not want to add legal complications to my already rapidly disintegrating life. It had become so bad that I began to apologise to him for every bruise or injury that was caused by him, and with no support network around, I didn't realise how foolish that actually was. I apologised to him for making him lose sleep that night as he sat at the emergency room and he said, "At least you had a bed."

The proverbial straw that broke the camel's back came to fruition one night in September of 2016 when the assault extended to my mother who was trying to videotape him while he was trying to strangle me with my seven-year-old screaming and hollering at what she was subjected to witness. I'll never be able to explain the courage or the reason why I picked up the phone and called the police that night. The police intervened and had him removed from the house for forty-eight hours. To people not familiar with abuse and how it works, it is probably the worst thing that can happen. No one is allowed to control the abuser, especially not his victims. I wasn't sure about what was going to happen when he returned - fear, mixed with hope that he might now change because he was caught in the act. Hope that maybe he really loved me and the innocent children that he would finally change. The fairy-tale did not end that way. The emotional abuse did not end, and almost on a daily basis he would tell me, "A wife should submit, the Bible says so. You call yourself a Christian?"

Those words were being painfully branded into my brain and I kept replaying the night the police entered the house. A male officer walked in ready to draw his gun and the female officer was just behind, but what I'll never forget was watching my abuser sitting so calmly on the sofa while I was visibly shaking and the children were screaming and crying. The split-second transformation from a raging maniac who had tried to strangle me to a picture of calm sitting on the sofa amazed me, but not the police, who had him forcefully removed from the property for two days. Everyone who heard about the incident told me, "You overreacted. He just got angry. I'm sure he didn't mean to hit you. We know that he didn't intend to strangle you. It's nothing. You shouldn't make such a big deal about, he just lost control."

I refused to believe it, and for the first time in my marriage decided to think for myself. I couldn't understand how someone, apparently so out of control could suddenly control himself when the police walked in. His body language just did not match the situation; he was not red in the face, visibly angry or even flushed in the face. He was just so normal and that's when a light bulb came on.

CHAPTER 15

GODLY SUBMISSION

This was not a man who lost control, this was a chronic abuser. This was ABUSE. This was the first time I had used that word to describe my marriage. I was being abused into submission. My mental state had been ripped out and slowly poisoned till I no longer knew or remembered who I was. I had lost my identity and had not fulfilled a single one of my own dreams. There was clearly some disconnect from what I believed I was to what I was reduced to. This was far from what I thought my life was going to be. I had dreams that were shattered and my abuser repeatedly said that an ignorant and stupid person like me wasn't smart enough to follow those dreams or even have those dreams

Here was a man who had taken extensive time to get to know me. He always told me, "I am excellent at reading people," and I now understood what he meant. He read me like a book from the first time we started talking. He made me trust him and share every single thing about my life, while he kept his cards extremely close to his chest.

After nearly ten years of marriage, I still don't know a single thing about his school life, college life, friends, relatives or even where his sisters live because he made sure that he kept me isolated from his entire family. It went to the extent that he even controlled every conversation I had with his family and had to be in his presence or on the speakerphone. And yet, he entitled himself to my family and their dinner parties without me. I had no say in anything throughout my marriage because he was the self-proclaimed intelligent one who was bringing in the money. The fact that I was bringing in exactly the same salary was insignificant, and I had allowed it to be that way.

This sounded extremely foolish to me now that I was out of the relationship, but looking back I could see how easy it was to fall into this trap. The smooth-talking charmer had won the hearts of everyone, and now he was undefeatable. This man had read me so well that he discovered the monster living in my head and they had become allies. They were working together and were rapidly destroying me. They both had the same goal and needed the same outcome, they wanted to destroy me, but not in a quick and easy manner. They needed to slowly destroy me, draining away at my energies and removing any self-worth and the will to fight. Their victory would never taste sweet if I was destroyed on their first try. My light bulb moment let me see that. My husband was not an out of control maniac, he was a strategising egomaniac whose goal was to victimise and burn me, while all along acting like the burn victim. There was nothing he wanted to see more than to break a woman who was deemed strong, courageous and confident and watch her crumble to pieces that nothing could ever fix.

Godly submission never involves tearing someone's self-worth to shreds. Godly submission needs to reflect how God sees us. It never involves any form of degradation because a person who submits is not considered weak in God's eyes. It takes a strong person to submit and submission doesn't mean you're weak or worthless. Submission doesn't make you a doormat for someone to wipe their feet on you. Biblical submission doesn't seem to be rightly understood. Biblical submission is where I choose to voluntarily put my trust in someone's authority and acknowledge their leadership. Again, leadership doesn't mean being a bully.

Leadership is respect on a two-way street.

(Please note, this book has no inclination toward a political context. I am only speaking on Godly submission in a relationship perspective).

So, then we need to define authority. It is NOT coercion, or slavery or suppression or a place to assert dominance. It is where someone voluntarily takes up the responsibility to care and provide for the other's needs, and that must include emotional, mental and psychological needs, along with any physical needs. A marriage needs to be based on this, and I think some of the marriages falling out are when the basics of this have been ignored or misguided. There is also the major aspect that's forgotten - that submission and authority in marriage are interchangeable. The only time they refuse to be interchanged is when there is abuse or harassment because the abuser can never see themselves in a position of submission and that's the red flag of an unhealthy relationship. In any healthy relationship, the strengths of one person complement the other and sometimes the person who is submissive in one area may take an authoritative role in another and there's a power balance. A relationship can never work if the power balance is constantly tipped in one direction because that doesn't allow the relationship to flourish. Any healthy relationship has an unstated goal, to help each other to be the best they can and keep the relationship fruitful. If one person constantly feels robbed of their potential and their dreams, then there's a negative power balance. The key lies in the realisation that there must be a power balance. Every strength or ability needs to be used to bond the family closer and build trust. Submission is an act of love and that is where abusers tend to contort the truth.

Submission is not founded on fear or force.

If you are submissive because you feel trapped, then you're probably being abused. The man doesn't need to physically hurt you for it to be called abuse. Experience taught me that abusers will use any available tactic to force you into submission. My abuser chose psychological abuse and manipulation and twisted and contorted everything that was said and happened to the extent that I began to doubt my sanity and finally ended up being called clinically depressed because I was certain I was losing my mind. It spiralled into rampant sexual and physical abuse, but began so subtly that I couldn't see it. I could not delineate reality and fiction any longer. It was exactly what he wanted to do, and now he had another arrow in his quiver where he could tell everyone that I was going insane and what a useless mother I was going to be.

It took several sessions and hours of marriage counselling with an astute psychologist before I actually saw what was staring at me in the face. He came along to one session and told her, "I don't know what you're trying to achieve from this session. There's no problem with me or the marriage." She did not back down and was very confident in how she dealt with him, and when I met with her privately, she told me that he displayed narcissistic characteristics. Being a student of psychology I knew that narcissism was one of the harder mental illnesses to diagnose. I had extensively read about it but I was overwhelmed by the fact that I had missed what I had lived with for nearly ten years.

I'm not going to indulge in the various research published or other empirical studies, but I'm discussing the simplest form of understanding this mental illness through my education and experience and how I learned to cope.

Narcissism is a 'sense of self-grandiosity' and that may be because of various reasons. It might be learned behaviour due to cultural background or upbringing, or it might serve as a way to cover up shame. Typically a narcissist lacks empathy and doesn't see others as emotional beings, but as objects that can be moved to suit their convenience. A narcissist only sees their needs at the forefront and that is at the cost of relationships. Being married to a narcissist put me squarely into the list of longing for an emotional connection, unable to express myself or my needs and a complete loss of self-worth. I discovered that I experienced a cycle of emotions, where I wanted out, but maybe if *he* would just change or show me a bit more attention then I wouldn't leave. Narcissists are emotional bullies who protect their true self by wielding malignant weapons of manipulation and hostility.

They simply cannot understand the repercussions of their actions or behaviour, for example, my abuser chose not to understand why I was so upset that he had hidden his bank statements or kept me isolated from everyone, and he believed that he was meeting the basic needs of the family, like having a job. He would constantly engage in *gaslighting*, as his easy mode of manipulation which made me distrust my perception of reality and sanity.

The term gaslighting originated from a film adaptation Gaslight where a man deliberately dims the gaslight in the house to convince his wife that she is imagining the light being dimmed. This was all an extensive ploy to convince her and others that she is insane through subtle manipulation to destroy her sense of reality, because he wanted to hide his murderous crime.

I began to see the reality of this only after I had freed myself from his vile manipulative clutches. He was a text book abuser whose ultimate goal was to make me second guess everything that had happened or was said. He worked hard to convince me that I had misheard him or that maybe I was growing old so didn't really hear him correctly. One incident I had with him was the perfect example of this. He tried to convince the police officers who came home that night when he hit me and tried to strangle me that he wasn't violent at all. He kept repeating, "I didn't raise my hands on her. I'm not a person like that. You can ask anyone. She set me up." It was eventually the bruises on me and my mother that convinced the police officers. Even before he was ordered to leave the house he told me, "I showed you all the bank statements. You are lying that you haven't seen it. You're setting me up to go to jail." He piled guilt on me with a blatant lie

Financial abuse was his next go to, where he made sure that I would be left penniless, which he brought to reality. His sense of entitlement was so great that when my lawyer asked him how he could live with himself by leaving his wife and two young kids with twenty dollars, he replied, "She chose the separation." His reply had no connection or sense as to why the situation had landed where it had, but it was this twisted manipulation that my eyes were slowly opened to. I began to see through the smoke and mirrors and finally saw him for who he was. He was an abuser who had forced me to submit to his authority and had put himself in that position through sheer force and degradation. His self-declared authority let him behave any way he liked and his abuse left me no option but to submit. He fed on the culture where we were brought up in. He used his *male* advantage to get what he wanted. Sexual consent meant nothing to him; it didn't matter before marriage and it surely didn't matter after we were married. *No* was not a word that went down well with him. He would sulk, but he gradually realised that sulking did not really feed his ego, so forcing me into submission was his only plan. He would persistently ask me if I had slept with other men and if that's why I didn't want to sleep with him. The first time I heard that felt like a slap to the face and I was torn emotionally and physically between rebellion and caving in. He felt no guilt in the way he was getting his authority recognised and yes, I realised it every single day, but getting out was not an option, not then.

I had to come to the revelation in the depths of my soul that he didn't care if he was liked by me, but he had to be admired because admiration outweighs likeability. He followed the typical pattern of lacking intellectual and genuine empathy, which meant, he probably knew he was hurting me and the people around, but he didn't really care because his behaviour didn't directly disadvantage him. He sat on the broad spectrum of narcissistic abusers because not all narcissistic abuse is created equal.

There are varying degrees of this, and in my case, it started with emotional and psychological abuse and finally escalated into physical. I had to come to the realisation that he didn't really understand relationships and the only scale he saw was *perfect* and *defective*. He saw me as *perfect* at the start of the relationship because he had something new to chase after and since narcissists typically do not have a middle ground, he saw my flaws like cute quirks. He spent enormous amounts of time and energy to convince me that I was the perfect match for him. He got a rush off the chase and once I was *caught*, every idiosyncrasy became a glaring flaw. He seemed to genuinely fall in love with me and kept me on the highest pedestal possible and although it seemed odd to me that he could fall in love with me after only a few phone conversations, I didn't think too much of it then. Had I spent a few more brain cells there, I would have seen that what goes up must come down, and I came down crashing. He saw me as a *renovator project* and was constantly telling me what I needed to do to look better or be better so I could match his status.

I was left bewildered because I didn't understand what changed, and the changeover was so subtle, I genuinely cannot pinpoint the exact incident of what changed. It is important to understand that every relationship deals with disappointment and in a *normal* relationship there is more or less peace being made with the reality that there are parts to both parties in the relationship that will always be less than ideal. It is very different from a narcissistic relationship, where the disappointment is seen as an insult to the narcissist and this angers them.

I remember the fights that escalated quickly into various realms of abuse because I displeased him. The criticisms were never constructive, they were downright insulting.

It took me to step out of the marriage to understand that he had a warped concept of marriage. He expected me to *submit* to him when he told me what I should wear, or whom I was allowed to talk to or even what to eat. He was ashamed to have me as his wife and I saw it when he took me to his workplace and made me sit in the far corner by the lifts and left me to watch his female colleagues greet him with hugs while I sat un-introduced beside the rubbish bin. I sat there left feeling utterly humiliated which made me storm off and when he returned home, he was furious that I had stormed out and ruined his reputation in front of his colleagues. Bewildered, and that incident, among the thousands of others left me apologising for my behaviour and saw me slink further down in his assessment of me. This was abuse. I began to realise that he had close relationships with his mother and sisters, but his demeaning way of treating them and controlling what career his sisters chose showed me that he was subjected to an abusive father. He even made one of his sisters decline to sign an important document with *her* husband because he hadn't seen it and it destroyed part of her relationship with her own husband.

He fit the profile that the son absorbs the disrespect that was shown to the female members of his family by the abusive father. His father had refused to visit the hospital at the birth of his middle daughter because he was disgusted that it was a girl and that same disgust flooded over to when my own daughter was born. His father's first words to me over the phone after I had given birth were, "Why did you give birth to a girl?"

I laid out the trends of the anecdotal information I had of his father and everything I knew of him and in a fury to understand what I had missed and how I could have missed this, I realised that the similarities were glaringly and frighteningly similar. Both of them did not really take any interest in the actual work required to bring up the children, yet they strongly believed that they were the authority on parenting. They considered themselves as the guiding force on parenting, even if that meant him hitting our daughter who was five at the time, hard across her face and then saying that this is what she should expect if her behaviour continued, and all she had done was screw up her face. I did get into a screaming match with him for hitting our daughter but to this day, I wonder if I could have done anything more. I realised that both these men never lost control; they took control of their partners and children, and me as the daughter in law. Every time I was in their house, his father would enter my room and dictate what I needed to wear and I had to simply oblige. His father felt entitled to every female around him.

Moving to a more sensitive topic, something that I had refused to acknowledge or think about right until this time that I was typing this book, was sex. My ex-husband wanted it entirely on his terms or not at all, and that meant, I had no say about it. Saying no to him was not a wise option either. I should have run a mile away from him at the first instance he chose to force himself on me. If I lived on all the *could haves and would haves and should haves*, my sanity would be a thing of the past and, the actual purpose of writing this book would have been defeated. This is exactly what I want you to know, as the reader, either as an abused person or you know someone going through abuse that this is not in your control.

It never was your problem, so trying to figure out where you went wrong is probably the worst injustice you can do to yourself.

I read from John Bevere: "God calls us to honour all those He has put in authority—but what do you do when authority asks you to do something that would be disobedience to God? The answer is simply this—the Bible teaches unconditional submission to authority, but CONDITIONAL obedience. Shadrach, Meshach, and Abednego honoured the king while at the same time refusing to bow down and worship him. Honour is unconditional. Obedience to authority has to align with God's Word."

Remember that the first human right the abuser takes away from you is the right to be angry. My marriage started falling apart the day I discovered an ex-girlfriend texting him, the pornography he was watching and that he had several bank accounts that he was hiding from me (the exact number I've never discovered till today),and that was nine years before my marriage actually crumbled. I chose to hide it from the eyes of the world, because what kind of wife would go around telling everyone about her cheating husband?

Every single thing that he twisted to suit himself was to force me into submission. I would try to convince him about how he manipulated everything and his denial would drive me to the point of insanity. It took me a couple of years of studying about the abusive narcissist to realise that in essence, they are all the same. They use the same smoke and mirrors to blind their behaviour, but in the end, the tactics are all the same. His lies were out of this world, and since there was no way for me to corroborate them or even prove his lies, his version was always held up because he portrayed himself as the rational one.

The hardest part of the marriage was the façade I was forced to wear every Sunday into the church. He would make me walk into church like we were the perfect couple despite his emotional and psychological abuse just an hour ago that left me red-faced and shaking in anger, while he was in perfect control.

This was another one of my lightbulb moments, where I realised that I had strived too long and hard to figure out what was wrong with me and what about me disgusted him, instead of trying to figure out what was wrong with him.

It is a very common mistake that the abused victims tend to make because everyone else thinks the abuser is absolutely fantastic. So it must be the victim's problem and the agony of this disparity can be gut-wrenching and you might be left in the same place I was, asking yourself *why me* over and over again. This is probably the control and isolation tactic best used by abusers because I felt I couldn't reach out to anyone. I mean, who would believe me, when I seemed like the crazy one who is so upset, while he's the calm rational face of the marriage? No one saw the abuser in him except me, and that automatically put me on the back foot. He would downplay and outright lie about every blowout we had and I could feel my brain cells dying. It took me out of my marriage to discover that he had been having affairs all through the nine years of marriage, something I had doubted since his ex-girlfriend texted him, and yet he would blow me away yelling, "What are you talking about? Do you have proof?" I replied, "I saw the message she sent you." Yet, my eyes were not proof enough for him, he wanted me to show him hard evidence of his affairs to convince him. He loved the fact that I had no hard proof of his affairs and somehow he had managed to twist all my relationships into sexual ones, whether it was male or female.

It was important for me to discover and come to terms that the abuse is cultivated from the values and belief system he was exposed to from an early age. He was the perfect example of being able to assert his dominance without raising his voice. He was a master at twisting everything I said to make it sound like the most ridiculous things he ever heard and he was unrelenting. He would wait for me to shrink away in disgust or walk out in anger before calling me unreasonable, and that left me with not being able to talk to anyone about it because I didn't know how to or what to explain about everything that had happened.

The arguing got to the point where I was constantly frustrated, and it spilled out at times in family gatherings and they would always question, "Why is she overreacting? Look at him; he is so calm in the face of her insanity." *Insanity* - the perfect word. He loved it and would use it at every opportunity he got. "You are mental. Your own family thinks you are. Everyone knows how unreasonable you are." He was a master at the art of manipulation and when I finally managed to tame my rage after the separation and ask him about all the hundreds of thousands he had spent on his affairs, he said, "We're separated now. I don't need to answer anything to you. You can't control me." It always went back to control and that control should always be on his side.

I was blown away by his level of automatic assertion, dominance, and manipulation. It was astonishing that all he could see in the relationship was *control* or *be controlled*. I was also amazed at the group of cronies he had acquired within my own extended family. They were the same people who just a few months earlier seemed angry that he had hit me.

I think it is important that I address this nature of the abuser who not just isolates his partner, but also builds a support system from the same people that once were on her side. He needed to do this because it's getting harder for abusers to remain abusers without getting into trouble with the law, so therefore if he has enough of a support network around him, who is the law going to believe? I will never forget the reality of this when I sat at a church pastor's office for counselling with my abuser and the pastor saw me getting angry at his lies that just wouldn't end. The pastor looked at me and said, "Do you know if you go to court you will lose both the children? Look at how calm he is and you're just so angry."

I knew at that moment I was at the loneliest point of my life, and I also knew that ignorance about domestic violence was rampant, not just outside the church but also in it. The pastor said it with the best intentions, but his ignorance of abuse made me lose trust in finding help anywhere outside of God. It was probably the best thing because I could go away and understand that the church was extremely well equipped to handle marital problems or a mutual separation or divorce, but the church was in no way equipped to handle abusive relationships. Everyone thought that they were well equipped to handle violence in families and that it probably also didn't help that it was only a man who chose to *counsel* and there was no female intervention there to understand both sides of the story.

What was more astonishing was the fact that I saw this a little too late. None of this added to godly submission. It was abuse and every kind of abuse in varying degrees.

CHAPTER 16

GRATITUDE IS MY CHOICE

"Cultivate the habit of being grateful for every good thing that comes to you, and to give thanks continuously. And because all things have contributed to your advancement, you should include all things in your gratitude." **Ralph Waldo Emerson**

If I reflect on my own situation, I was thrown into a pit of isolation by the love of my life and was left there to die. An illusion of respite appeared when an extended family member chose to intervene and hear my side of the story. She listened quietly as I confided in her and she said she felt sorry for my situation and was empathetic that I was left bruised and battered, but here's the challenge… she never saw it. She never saw the nights I cried myself to sleep because I was wondering if I was going insane. She never saw the night where he had his hands around my neck trying to choke me. She only saw him as a persona of calm and had only heard of the violent attack from me. Her intervention went to the extent of building a twisted relationship with my abusive ex-husband under the ploy of *helping the children*. That game was uncovered when she came to tell me, in front of my children, "You were the cause of the abuse... and there was no real abuse." As ridiculous as it sounds, it seemed to make perfect sense to her, because she had never seen the abuse... so obviously, how could there be abuse? She had seen the smiling and the hand holding and we had not one, but two children, so surely there was no problem in the marriage. The most ridiculously absurd statements she said were, "Well, if you were suffering, why didn't you tell me before? Why didn't you just leave? Why did you have two children? No abused lady would have another child with an abuser." With that, she had poisoned my children's psyche without realising the consequences of her words, consequences I'm still processing and trying to fix years later.

If you've been in any sort of abusive relationship, you know these sentences would make your skin crawl. The ignorance lathered with arrogance made my blood boil because the damage those words cause are sometimes irreparable.

Ignorance about abuse and arrogance about the level of knowledge people have about domestic abuse is probably the worst concoction. People believe that abuse does happen, but cannot believe that abused women can have decent paying jobs or a decent education. The arrogance that says that only uneducated women can be abused or that only women who come from a vulnerable and low socio-economic status are victims is the poison that is slowly killing our society.

Like Joseph, I had to go through the pit and the prison before I knew what freedom actually looked like. I was distraught then, but now I can say that I am grateful for every hurt caused, intentionally or otherwise. I am grateful for every time I heard, *"Why are you still with him? Why didn't you tell us before that you were violated? Are you lying?"* I was dealing with some of the hardest questions and then being forced to cower in shame from the same people I trusted. I am grateful that I heard, *"How can you say that your own husband abused you? Maybe you did something and pushed his buttons?"* I am grateful that my every last bit of trust in people was destroyed. If it weren't for the crudeness of people, I never would have tasted freedom. I had to go through the emotions myself and had to summon the courage to face the reality of my now dead marriage. It made me look at my situation completely differently and I don't think there was a greater injustice done, than what I was doing to myself by replaying every hurt over and over again. I could almost feel the bile climb up my oesophagus every time I thought of the betrayal, and then I reflected back to my revelation of gratitude. It was not a natural response. I had to choose to *give thanks in all circumstances; for this is God's will for you in Christ Jesus* (1 Thessalonians 5:18). If it weren't for the people who ended up destroying me when they thought they were helping me, I never would have discovered the destiny God had planned for me. Personally, I believe that the Bible was far ahead of its times, and God wanted us to experience the power of praise.

What I chose to focus on determined my destiny.

I realised that it's easy to have faith like Jacob had at Bethel when you know God is physically in that place, it's a lot harder when I was faced with uncertainty. Praise was the key along with submission. God just could not do anything without me submitting to Him. I had to realise that my healing was going to come in the way God ordained it and that was what submission was. I trusted myself voluntarily into God's hands and let Him decide on how my healing should happen because it wasn't until much later when I realised that God had others to heal through my pain. I needed to understand submission in the purest sense, and the struggle that comes with godly submission. Godly submission is worldly submission flipped on its head. I had to entrust everything I knew into His hands. I had to accept that I didn't know as much as I thought I did and I had to willingly entrust everything into heaven's hands. I had to humble myself to submit and experience taught me that the monsters in my mind were also the worst windbags ever encountered. The battle was and still is an everyday thing.

Humility is not a natural but a necessary response.

It took every fibre in my being to go against what I was normally conditioned to and accept that God's word in the Bible was the ultimate truth. *"Humble yourselves, therefore, under God's mighty hand, that he may lift you up in due time"* and 1 Peter 5:6 says, *"Humble yourselves before the Lord, and he will lift you up"* and James 4:10, both spoke about humility. That was a promise and accepting the word of God as my foundation for living was harder than I'd like to accept. I thought that I truly believed that the Bible was God's word, but being confronted with it showed me that I only chose to believe some of it. Verses that required anything from me were the hardest to digest. Looking back, Psalm 91 is a great Psalm and speaks about God's ever-loving nature and protection over every aspect of my life, but I chose to ignore verse 1 because it required something from me. *"Whoever dwells in the shelter of the Most High will rest in the shadow of the Almighty."* It meant **I had to dwell** in the shelter of God, which meant it was a choice I had to make.

The same was with Psalm 23, another awesome Psalm that speaks about the guiding grace of God and how He will put my enemies to shame before me. All that was mine *if,* the Lord was my shepherd. That sounds easier to read than to live because it meant that I was now a sheep who trusted my shepherd to provide my every need. This was again the uncomfortable part that required me to trust God completely, not just in areas that I struggled with. The true test of my submission to God was in areas that were my strength. Could I ask God for guidance in things I did well? This was unnatural, but I knew that true godly submission meant doing exactly that.

He needs us to be humble at all times and I learned that if I struggle to submit my strengths to God, then I still have pride.

Submit to the Lord - when we submit to God, we see ourselves as much more than what we think we are. God doesn't belittle us or treat us as slaves… He helps us see that we are a little lesser than angels and that's pretty high up the pecking order. The results may or may not be realised on earth and I had to be ok with that. I will not pretend to know the answers to what goes on in the heavens, because it has taken me a journey through the pits and prisons of life before I realised that I do not have enough faith to live life without God.

There are questions constantly brewing in me about everything that has happened to me. I've always asked myself and asked God, *"Why was I susceptible to depression? Why did I go through what I did? Was I too dumb to miss the obvious?"* I had to go through the Bible before I realised, that's not how God works. He doesn't answer everything, because some things are meant to stay unanswered. Just like any good parent, it does sometimes feel that He is cruel, but sometimes He has to be cruel to be kind, so it's not really cruelty, is it? God has not given me a reply for my questions, but he has given me a revelation of who He is. That alone has taken me farther in my journey than I possibly envisioned.

Looking back to Joseph's life, he went through the journey of betrayal, pit and prison and more betrayal before he realised why he had gone through his pain. Some have argued that God could have brought Joseph to the realisation that he was chosen to save God's people through a less painful and traumatic story, but there is a key thing here. Focussing on godly submission and to accept that God knew the best way to bring Joseph to this revelation and only God knows the number of people in centuries and millennia ahead that would draw strength from Joseph's story. If it were any other way, I probably would have no way to relate to what was going on in my own life. Relying on God's wisdom was another challenge, and I deeply believe that God understands our challenge. He understands my constant questioning where, firstly I can't see Him and secondly, how do I know what I'm going through is God's plan?

I think we can all take courage in the story of Job. God had control of his life all along, and I think if it were not for the stories of the heroes of the Bible, I would have struggled to cope with my journey. I fully appreciate the magnitude of their struggles because I drew strength from it, and I think only God could have known that centuries in advance. I grew to appreciate the true side of Christianity - it is built on submission, and no wonder the enemy's main goal is to warp what God established. The enemy has twisted submission into control and abuse and Christianity into a religion. It was never intended to be a religion. Jesus proved that by dispelling all the religious theories the Pharisees had.

Jesus came to show that religion can't really take us very far because religion goes hand in hand with condemnation and a judgemental attitude. He wanted us to see Christianity as a relationship not as a religion, because with a relationship comes love. Romans 8 verse 1 explains that, *"Therefore, there is now no condemnation for those who are in Christ Jesus."* Then it goes on to show God's love for us by sending Jesus to us. It was a massive journey for me to realise that love was what God was about, and always has been. He has not changed from the Old Testament to the New Testament. I had to submit wholly to Him to truly understand His love and to be able to speak as the three men thrown in fire did, *'Whether I survive this or not doesn't matter, I still know He's on the throne.'* There was a linear relationship going on, submission was engulfed in gratitude and then wrapped in self-worth. The core of it was submitting to Him and that opened my life to a whole world of possibilities. What the world thought of me did not determine my destiny or my self-worth. My self-worth was determined in heaven when Jesus died for me and no one was going to rob me of that. In saying that, gratitude goes hand in hand with submission.

Getting out of that vicious cycle was not as simple as I thought, and to be honest, I think I still come face to face with the monster at times, only now, I'm able to look it in the eye instead of cowering away and being ashamed of myself. I do feel its icy claws now and then beginning to wrap around my thoughts, but I found the greatest weapon that I can use to paralyse its grip before it gets too tight. I have to look at the monster in its cold bloodthirsty eyes and tell it one thing I'm grateful for.

Gratitude is not a natural response, it is a willing attitude.

I had to rummage through the pits of my heart to find things I was grateful for. I had to *make a deliberate declaration of gratitude*. The monster never begins by screaming the injustices done, because then I would know it was the monster. It was never going to play the easy game. The voice of the monster is so subtle and often sounded like my own. I heard things like, '*Those kids are making such a mess in the house and all you've been doing is cleaning up after them.*' I had to be extremely vigilant of its voice. This sentence may seem normal but then it can spiral out of control. I had to step on a higher ground and beat the inner voice with my mouth, *"I'm grateful I have children who are normal and make a mess. I'm grateful for my kids."*

I could almost hear it slither away. The victory was adrenaline charged. I was elated. For the first time, I didn't have to listen to the hiss of the monster sucking my self-worth as it chuckled darkly. I had won!

The monster doesn't stop, and from experience, I don't think it ever will but the good thing is, I am extremely familiar with its voice and can get away from its grip quicker each time. The trick is to not let my guard down. It's not always easy. Sometimes the monster is relentless and I did end up caving in but refused to beat myself about it. I was not designed to beat this monster every time. There are times when I didn't want to think about victory, and the defeated feeling felt a little too familiar. Those were some of the darkest points when I believed that victory didn't matter anymore. I was back where I started and felt that I was in a worse situation than when I had tasted my first victory. I knew what victory felt like and just couldn't bring myself to beat the monster again. I writhed under its grasp for days, losing focus of my purpose as I let it beat my self-worth out of me. I knew that I had to taste the victory again. I began to write in a little book every single thing I was grateful for.

Every time I heard the monster begin to speak in a hiss like whisper, I had an arsenal of ammunition that I could throw at it. I carried that book around because gratitude needs to be deliberate. That was the only thing that would remove the venom from the monster's fangs. Every time the grip around my neck got tighter, I began to speak everything I was grateful for. The battle is a never-ending one where I had to fight for my self-worth because there are constant elements that are waiting to strip the dignity away, and, unfortunately, my mind was one of them.

I didn't understand how I had made the connection to speak gratitude into the monster's hold. I believe that the battle strategy was in its simplest, most crude form where I just had to do the opposite of what the monster did. I had to negate the effect of its voice and the only weapon I had was to speak the opposite of negative...positive. I had to also use the opposite medium and needed to vocalise the positive words. I had to do the opposite of the monster's tactics. I couldn't fight it in its stronghold. It was too powerful there, I had to rise to a higher place and use a more powerful battleground... my *spoken* words. I couldn't speak positive words in my mind, because that was the monster's home. I had to step out in the open because the monster doesn't like the light. I had to gain altitude over this monster that was determined to defeat me on its terms. I went a step further, might seem like a no-brainer to most Christians, but this was the hardest next step I had to take. I began praising God. I've heard countless preachers talk about praising God and I reflected theologically about how I was praising God through my actions as well. I realised all that was an add-on to what God truly intended. He knew the weapon that had the most power and that was simply and genuinely praising out loud. I needed to get out of my fear of displeasing God and worrying about what God might think about me. I began to wonder if God thought, *'How dare such a worthless worm praise the Almighty God? Does she think she's even worthy to raise her hands to Me and what makes her think I'll even listen?'*

This was a familiar thought because that was the whisper I had lived with every time I tried to seek God. I had to get over my fear of failing to be a perfect Christian. I had to come to the realisation that there was no such thing as the perfect Christian. It was a test of enduring the storm and the billowing waves. The fear of failure set me back from seeing the reality of what I knew deep down but was too scared to acknowledge.

I had to see failure was put there, so I could grow. I needed that failure to see the lessons that it would teach me and that made me forcibly change the way I looked at every situation.

Perfection was never a criterion for His love.
Gratitude is not determined by the circumstances that surround me.

Gratitude is a choice I have to make every day, and my experience in psychology and empirical studies have shown the benefit of gratitude on the human brain. Research has been conducted on the effects of gratitude

(Emmons & McCullough, 2003) (Zahn, et al., 2009) on people with mental health issues and the way it positively shaped the neural pathways by increasing serotonin and dopamine, or the 'happy chemicals'. Years of research by multitudes of researchers and psychologists revealed that expressions of gratitude through letters impact neural activity positively (Kini, Wong, McInnis, & Ga, 2016) and let people sleep better and they had a direct impact on depression symptoms. God said that in His word centuries ago. I appreciate that there is a deeper research done than just what the Bible describes, but the essence is found in 1 Thessalonians 5:16-18, *"Giving thanks in everything..."* Giving thanks or being grateful is a learned skill and it took a lot of heartaches for me to realise that this is unnatural and that's precisely why I must do it.

Setting my self-worth right was my priority and there were prolonged periods of self-reflection that I needed to do. I had to submit myself to God which meant seeing myself how He saw me and submitting to accepting what He saw. I needed to see that I was perfect in the eyes of God and that's all that mattered.

I gradually began to understand God was really not disappointed in me just because I did not fit the silhouette of the perfect Christian according to the church. I slowly understood the mind the prophet Samuel had spread to the modern day church. It was not easy to accept someone who was not the same stature as their last renowned leader Saul. You had to fit a certain profile, a certain upbringing, a certain qualification, a certain mannerism or you didn't fit at all. I understood now why my ex-husband was accepted everywhere he went. He fit the silhouette of a Saul, in his case, a future pastor. He fit the world and the church's measuring stick perfectly. I didn't. For example, I had a temper, but no one saw my daily battle as I worked through it. For example, the pastor who told me that I would lose my kids in a custody battle because of my temper had never actually seen me lose my temper. All he was going by was my ex-husband's words.

He had believed my ex-husband who gave the aura of perfection because he fit the measuring stick. He automatically decided that my ex-husband was perfect because in public view he seemed a better fit as a Christian. It was exactly like the prophet Samuel believed about Eliab who seemed more king-like than David (1 Samuel 16:6-7). Samuel was going by Eliab's public appearance and did not know the real Eliab who was haughty and condescending towards David (1 Samuel 17: 26-30), exactly like the pastor was going by my ex-husband's public display of perfection without knowing the skeletons in his closet.

I slowly began to understand that the modern church easily fell into the trap of exemplifying the same behaviour they preached against. I understood that the measuring stick used was one of man and not of God. That measuring stick made me struggle with wanting to serve in the church while my heart felt like it was ripped to shreds. How could I socialise with people from the church? How do I tell them about my struggles without feeling judged? How do I even begin to address the agony in my heart when I can't come to terms with it myself? I was forced to reach a level of maturity for myself and everyone else and where I was forced to bring out my iron-clad masks of perceived calm. I had to understand that people were stepping into my personal space, not with terrible intentions but they were trying hard to fit into the social measuring stick too.

I began to see that trying to fit into the social measuring stick was not my issue to fix. Just because I began to see myself through God's eyes, didn't automatically stop the enemy from trying to destroy my self-worth on a daily basis. The struggle is real, the battle is real, but it's easier now. I realised I was not alone in this battle. I had the *Military Genius* on my side and He knew the battlefield better than anyone else. I realised that I had to go through this battle because my story was important. My battle scars would bring healing to another wounded soldier and that made my battle necessary. I had to stop questioning God through this season of my life. I had to learn from the lives of the men in the Bible. God knew something was on the other side of the struggle that I couldn't see until I had reached there. I had to learn to submit to His will, and though I would rather have not had my struggle, I had to learn that if God thought there was a purpose in my pain, then I had to let Him lead me through it. I needed to learn the true meaning of Godly submission and trust God.

Faith played a massive role in this journey. It was one thing to say that I had faith in God, but it was a whole other thing to actually have that faith in God and trust Him through the pit and prison. It took immense willpower to accept that He was going to guide me through this and no matter how long or hard the journey, He knew better than I did. Accepting God's wisdom during the pain is a journey that I embark on daily. My human brain makes me look at the rational explanation and I have to deliberately change my thinking to accepting God's wisdom.

God tells us to be like a child and I finally understood what He meant when He said in Matthew 18 verses 3-5, [3] *"And he said: "Truly I tell you, unless you change and become like little children, you will never enter the kingdom of heaven.* [4] *Therefore, whoever takes the lowly position of this child is the greatest in the kingdom of heaven.* [5] *And whoever welcomes one such child in my name welcomes me."*

My precious children gave me the revelation that I could never have discovered myself. My little two year old boy had just started learning nursery rhymes and he was now absolutely fascinated by Little Miss Muffet. I watched him grab a little spoon and a bowl and that was his *'curds away'* (curds and whey). He just could not get enough of the song and sang it from the time he woke up to when I rocked him to sleep. That was almost twelve hours of non-stop Little Miss Muffet and it didn't bother him that I begged him to stop. Then my little nine year old got in on the action, so I now had two children singing Little Miss Muffet all day… everyday… and they still are while I type this paragraph.

I tried everything to get them to stop. I put on other nursery rhymes. I even told them that the song was silly, just to get them to stop singing it. Nothing changed their minds, and it took me over three weeks of listening to this song, and I was at my wits' end before I had this amazing revelation. God wanted me to see that NOTHING could change the fact that they were children and no amount of outside forces could rattle that. They were children who loved and were fixated on a nursery rhyme and that was all that mattered. I looked at my own life and I began to wonder what changed as I had grown up. Why were all the outside influences able to shift my focus so rapidly? This was exactly why Jesus said that only the children filled with their precious innocence would be able to inherit heaven, and that didn't necessarily mean get into heaven, it meant, make heaven come down.

I could not bring heaven down in all its power if I let the world make me believe that I couldn't. It was absolutely imperative for me to view my life as a child would, and that's not talking about being ridiculously carefree but it talks about how I see my place in heaven through God's eyes, and only His eyes. God was showing me, through my little children, that the cruel words, insults, ridiculous expectations of the world should not impact what I was destined for, or how God saw me. He had created me as who I was for a reason and had given me strengths, weaknesses, talents and gifts that were exclusive to me. There was never going to be another one like me and that was a deliberate plan of God. I watched the monster shrink away as I began to speak this truth out loud.

It took me to the verge of death, quite literally, before I saw precisely what God wanted me to see. He wanted me to see the wounded warriors surrounding me, and they were in the exact same situation as I was and they thought they were alone too. My battle scars meant I could show them that we can survive. I was grateful that they were scars because it meant that I had survived. I had a medium to connect with other warriors and they identified with the scars.

I was ashamed of my battle and I was ashamed of the scars that were extremely deep, both physically and emotionally because I felt like a failure. I had to learn that my scars were nothing to be ashamed of. I learned that from the Bible, in fact, everything I learned about the battles of life came from the Bible. King David taught me that there was no shame in showing your emotions or your scars. I learned that focusing on my weakness kept my focus away from my destiny. God knows our weakness and I think sometimes we are stuck with them for life, like Paul was with the thorn in his side, because that thorn provides healing for someone else. Making a conscious decision of gratitude showed me points in my life where I was the most hurt, but had to be the most grateful for.

I had to learn to thank God for every one of my abuser's groupies who fed off the gossip and my emotional instability because if it were not for them, I never would have discovered my self-worth doesn't depend on man's opinions. Thank God for the pastor who simply didn't *get it*. If it weren't for his ignorance in the area of abuse, I never would have found my peace and freedom in God without depending on human wisdom. Thank God for the cruel words I heard from so many family members because that showed me the true reality of the written word of God. Thank God for the police who made me go to victim support because I realised I wasn't alone. Thank God for that precious counselling centre because if I hadn't gone there, I never would have seen the greater need there and the charity BaG (Bring and Give) would not have been born.

I could choose to live in the past, and do myself no favours or choose to look ahead at what I had. Even my language needed to change and it was not an overnight transformation. I still struggle to choose gratitude in every situation and some days are harder than others, but choosing to be grateful does get easier. It's a life skill, the more you do it, the easier it becomes.

This is not just a theological concept; the positive effects of gratitude are being researched in great detail in the psychological faculties too. Research has proved the positive effect of choosing gratitude as a medium of therapeutic intervention (Emmons & Stern, 2013). King David's famous son King Solomon, who had experienced life probably more than any man, with riches more than that could be measured, and wisdom to match wrote in Proverbs 18:21, *"The tongue has the power of life and death, and those who love it will eat its fruit."*

This tells me that my words have a greater impact than I'd like to admit. I can choose to live in the agony of the past pain and know full well the impact that was going to have on my mental health or choose to be grateful for what I have and allow peace into my life.

It is not the easiest or the quickest way to deal with agony, because my dirtbag brain would relive every single traumatic event a hundred times daily to the point where I was left in a crumbling heap on the floor. It was also extremely important to remember that the monster is living inside my mind and has not gone away. It still does veer its head quite often, but having the knowledge of the weapons in my arsenal makes it easier to shrink its power quite quickly. In saying that, there are some days where the attack is more surreptitious and that makes it harder to detect, but it is imperative for me to understand that this is a battle.

It was not a one-time victory, winning over mental illness never is. It just meant that I needed to make a decision that I was going to fight this monster, no matter how long it takes and I was going to win.

There is a greater destiny and my greatest weapon is my story.

My wounds are some of the greatest artillery because I know that they are meant to bring healing to someone. I think Jesus chose to die the way He did, in utter brutality and disgrace, humiliated and nailed to the cross, to show us His wounds. This was the essence of what He first showed His disciples and then again what He showed Thomas when He said, *"Put your finger here; see my hands. Reach out your hand and put it into my side"* (John 20:20-27). He wanted us to display our scars boldly because only through your scars can healing come to someone else. Isaiah 53:5 captures that beautifully, *"... and by his wounds we are healed."* We need our scars. They are worth more than you can ever imagine.

Your scars are someone's destiny.

It was important for me to love myself as Jesus did, because I would never see myself as the perfect image He had created and just that lack of knowledge made me lose to that monster. I had to learn to be kind to myself. It is an everyday process. It's a constant battle and each day that you are kind to yourself, the monster shrinks away.

Whether people approved of me or not didn't really matter, I was still important to God. Everything about me was important to Him and His purpose on earth. Reading Hebrews 4:16 showed me why I needed to be confident in who I was, *"Let us then approach God's throne of grace with confidence, so that we may receive mercy and find grace to help us in our time of need."* The cause of mental struggles itself shouldn't be my only focus, but it meant that my depression and struggles with mental illness were a greater reason to draw closer to Him. Mental illness is a battle and often a lifelong one and yet, coming to the realisation of it was going to be my greatest ammunition.

FINAL NOTE FROM THE AUTHOR

You may be young or old; you may have a strong inclination to faith and God or may be agnostic or an atheist. Are you a human being who has gone through a traumatic event like violence, assault for example (I use these as examples simply because of my experience), or abuse (and please remember it doesn't have to be physical or sexual to be called abuse)? And maybe you are suffering from depression as a result of that trauma, or maybe you can't really find a reason or an explanation for your depression or unexplained anxiety. Maybe you have self-harmed or thought about it; maybe you have thought about suicide or even attempted to take your life. Are destructive thoughts eating you up? Do you feel like the weight of the world is crushing you and that no one can see your life being squeezed out of you? You may have a support network or you may not. You may have a therapist or you may believe that not even a therapist could fix you. Do you find yourself in isolation and constantly hearing a voice that mocks who you are? Does that voice question your self-worth? Does that voice make you feel worthless and that nothing you do or achieve will ever bring you to meet the standards of the world? Does that voice constantly scream at you that the world would be a better place without you? Are you climbing a road in your life that is so steep that it feels like you're walking on jagged rocks and each time you fall they cut through you?

If you've been in one or any of these situations, then I'm here to tell you that you matter. I may have never met you and neither of us knows the other, but your life matters to me. I was in the same situation dealing with all the above and more and thought I needed to hide myself because I believed I was worth nothing. Then I discovered that I was not alone. You matter so much that I made the hardest decision to write this book knowing that it would expose my vulnerabilities. I chose to expose my weakness to the ever judging public eye in the form of this book, if only to reach you and let you know that you matter. You are worth more than what the world believes. The world is a cruel place that unfairly measures you against a yardstick that was handed to it. I want to let you in on a secret. You are never going to measure up to the world's measures and that's not a bad thing! That's what makes you… you! You're wanted; you're special… yes, with your struggles and all. You are so precious and your story will save someone so please don't be ashamed. Depression thrives in darkness… shine a light on it and watch it shrink away.

Mental illness like depression, anxiety or suicidal thoughts does not make you any less of a human being. It makes you a strong person for choosing to wake up every morning and fight the next day. It makes you stronger than those who judge you. Don't be ashamed of your scars.

Your scars are more valuable than your trophies.

I was brought up with a Christian faith, but there were times I was less than Christian. I wrote this book with a Biblical eye because that was all I had when I was left battered. I had isolated myself from every social contact except my professional circle, but I had no choice there. I began to wear a mask every day and as the days went by, I chose not to take it off and soon it became me. I had morphed into something I was a far cry from. I found vices that help me survive rock bottom, but only for the short term. I watched myself deteriorate as I took on a haggard look and I watched my life slowly drain away. I was deliberately sabotaging myself in isolation and at the same time drawing the iron curtains over who I really was.

It was easier to clown around and feign laughter than actually face the heartache. I chose to keep the skeletons locked away because I didn't want anyone to see my weaknesses. I was convinced, if I showed my vulnerabilities and if people saw me for who I really was, it would never be the same again. It just wouldn't be acceptable for my colleagues or for anyone to see the anxiety that sometimes left me clinging to the bathroom floor.

I came to the end of my tether when the anxiety attacks occurred more frequently and I couldn't keep up my façade any longer. My career could no longer be my safe space. The monster's grip around me tightened and I was gasping as I trembled and clung on to life, debating if it was easier to let the monster win. With two young children I had started to believe that it was not worth living. I just had to get out of here. The monster was winning and it was in an instant where it loosened its grip on me and I turned to the only thing that I had… the Bible. I did not want to talk to any human being and I believed that my safest space was alone. I realised how wrong I was when I read the Bible. You may or may not agree with my biblical perspective on this, but this book was not written to cause contention but was written to show that mental illness doesn't only affect the faint hearted. The monster portrays itself as colossal and feeds off your fear. The more scared you are of it, the bigger it grows. The monster eats away at you, one self-worth at a time, and one tear of agony at a time, one panic at a time, one worry at a time. The only way you are going to defeat this behemoth is by turning on the light. That means to shine a light in its eye to show people this monstrosity exists and watch it shrink before your eyes.

Telling one person… actually, let's start with telling yourself about this monster. Clear up some myths about it for your own sake. The monster has no victim profile. Stop telling yourself that this monster found you because you're weak and spineless. This monster found the strongest men and that's why I needed the Bible to reassure me of that. It found mighty kings like David and tremendously confident and powerful prophets like Elijah and the monster crippled them emotionally. They had to deliberately search to find the key to decapitating this monster and if you think the monster is getting too big for you, you are not alone. Everything in this book may not make sense, it doesn't have to. This book is simply a bridge that I believe will get you across the line to the place that you can and need to be at.

I realised from experience that it takes more than a minor inconvenience for someone to start contemplating suicide. Depression takes on many forms and doesn't need a specific trigger. It starts as small waves that brush against your feet and you can see glimpses of the monster peering from the waves. It watches you intently as its cunning tentacles slither over your spirit, slowly crushing it and you don't know that it's crushing you. It's too cunning to be spotted and you only see the monster's grip when it has its clutches around your neck and by now, it's squeezing the life out of you, and unfortunately for some people it can be too late.

It can hit you like a ton of bricks where you're fine one day and all of a sudden you're engulfed in a tsunami of emotions. The person who has a career, a mum, a dad, a sportsman, a doctor, a lawyer, and all those fantastic titles get thrown out the window as you are reduced to a crumbling heap crying for death or the earth to just open up and swallow you whole. You probably have thought frantically about your children, your pets, your friends and family or whoever is dear to you and how they would cope without you, but you hear the monster whispering, "They probably don't care. They'll be better off without your sad miserable presence."

This monster wants nothing more than to defeat you and unfortunately, it has succeeded on many instances. Its voice has just been too convincing and you can be certain that the monster has not set up a funeral to mourn the lives lost. It moves to the next person and whispers to them in blood lust. Do you remember the chatterbox voice at the beginning of the book? The voice that kept saying, "You're not good enough. You're not pretty enough. You're absolutely useless." That voice will destroy you. It is the voice that we too often give too much importance to and that voice dictates our self-worth. You know that God has created you as you and nothing you hear or say can change the fact that He values you more than life itself.

There's a reason why I wrote so extensively about each of the Bible figures. They each represent a familiar phase in our life where we have passed through or camped at for a significant time, but that's all it is… it's a camp, it's not your destiny. I wanted you to read each of the stories and see these struggles are not new and you are not alone. I have heard so many people say they have been horrible people who cannot fathom God ever forgiving them. But I am urging you to not live by the world's standards, because if repentance is pure, you have a fantastic destiny and eternity ahead.

Look at the life of David, he killed a person just so he could get that man's wife, and yet God only cared that his repentance was genuine and that he never sinned again. These men of faith were chosen by God not because they were free of sin, but because of their scars. I know that God's plan is to use your life and your disappointment, hurt and failure… those very things that you thought were your limitations. We are often haunted by feelings of hopelessness and guilt and that can be emotionally draining. In the case of a Christian, you believe that once you are saved, everything is brand new, and while for some it can be the case, for the majority of us, we're still faced with the ghosts that stay hidden in the walls of our heart. Struggling with the daily thoughts of inadequacies and wondering how on earth we can ever complete this race, can emotionally drain you fairly quickly.

It's essential that you realise who you really are. You were chosen to be put on this earth to reach your destiny because of the very flaws that you think will hold you back. Your inadequacies are exactly what will propel you to your destiny in Jesus. He understands everything you're going through better than anyone because He went through it all and He chose to bear the burden. He made himself weak before the world so you and I could gain strength through His weakness.

The only thing He wants is for each of us to see ourselves how He sees us. He doesn't see our scars as obstacles to our destiny. He wants us to wear our scars proudly because they are the gates to someone's healing. This was a lesson that took me a long time to comprehend and get my head around. I thought I needed to shrink away because I suffered from depression and anxiety, and I sometimes still do. I thought I needed to hide away from the view of the world, because I would be judged for my extreme anxiety that had morphed into a compulsion that sometimes left me doing several irrational things like flicking on the light switch for several minutes to the point that I looked like a lunatic to everyone.

I was faced with a two-fold struggle. First, I struggled with my mental illness and, second I struggled to hide my mental illness.

I began to feel crippled by this and I felt that I needed to fit into what was accepted, and I felt that I was not of the acceptable type. That's why writing this book was so important, because I did not choose to write this book to display my education or my theological effectiveness. I wrote this book because it was the only way of self-exploration I knew. This book was written in utmost humility because this was a gateway for me to see the truth to this struggle that almost cost me my life. I read a quote that resonated deeply with my intention of this book.

> *"The best part of writing is really to educate yourself. I don't want to be anybody's expert. I came in to learn."*
> *-Ta-Nehisi Coates*

Nothing has opened my eyes more to the dangers of suicide and mental illness than reading my own story from the outside.

We're reaching out wrong. They can't seek help.

I have been reading recent articles and media releases about famous people or celebrities committing suicide and how no one saw it coming. How they seemed like they were happy and normal and even spoke with such joy and how shocked everyone was that they had taken their lives. There have been countless hashtags of #ReachOut, #Seek Help across social media. We're asking the wrong end of the spectrum to reach out - we need to reach out first. We're again placing unneeded pressure on an already fragile mental state that we expect people struggling with mental health to reach out first. It's almost like blaming the victims for not reaching out first. It is the common sense of society to reach out first. We need to be so attuned to those around us for us to see the signs among our loved ones.

Suicide is not a disease affecting only the rich and famous, and why do we talk so extensively about reaching out when we have this monster gripping our near and loved ones? We need to have the astute ability to understand that the media is competing amongst each other, vying for top spot in coverage of a high profile suicide, but the same media will promote every negative aspect from body shaming to television shows glorifying suicide. We are fooling ourselves if we think that the entire media society is concerned about suicidal rates, or the high pandemic of mental illness impacting our society.

Mental illness doesn't care if you belong to a first world or third world country, the effect of the monster is the same and the monster living in our head is feeding off the monster in the media. We need to be the voice against promoting any negativity that is conducive to mental illness.

How can we in one breath, say that we are all for helping people struggling with mental illness, and in the same breath post a comment on social media about a person who doesn't measure up to our yardstick - be it looks, brains or even values? I can't in my right conscience say that I want to fight mental illness and yet tell someone who is of a different sexual orientation that God will punish them in hell. It is almost like us saying that we hate human or child trafficking, but we don't have a problem with pornography. Pornography is a catalyst. Pornography portrays a skewed version of sex and it's targeted to make men look at women as weak and someone who can be controlled. Women typically are seen as existent to only satisfy the needs of man. Is it any surprise that men who abuse have a large attachment to pornography as well? We have been trained to ignore the catalyst to the chemical reaction, and we don't even realise it. The Bible has been steering my thinking in the direction that was crucial to protecting my sanity. I finally understood what it meant when people say that the **Bible never goes out of style.** There was so much comfort and wisdom between the pages, and I can truly say that nothing else could have kept me alive though my journey.

On a final note though, my figurative journey through hell and death has been harrowing to say the least, it has been my greatest weapon in overcoming my fear of the unknown. I have realised that there truly is a God who loves me and who wants nothing more than to see me reach my destiny which was formed in heaven. I've learned lessons that I never thought I needed to. I learned about forgiveness and I've understood that forgiveness is the greatest gift that I can give myself. It has been a painful journey to come to that realisation, but I can look back and now I see that harbouring that anger and hatred towards my ex-husband and his family has done me absolutely no good. I think my journey through the pit has made me a little bit more Christ-like, although, it's a deliberate effort on my part to forgive every day. I can now say that I understand that it wasn't just me who was trapped in a life of abuse and manipulation; it was also my ex-husband. He is just as trapped as I was and unfortunately, it might be harder for him to choose to come out of the clutches because of the varying degrees of realisation. I was trapped and I knew I was trapped and I wanted to be free. Unfortunately for him, he may never accept that he's trapped because he has lost nothing by staying in his prison. He enjoys the seclusion and unless he sees that seclusion as isolation, then he's never going to seek freedom.

My journey has taught me to love my children like I never have before. I value every second with them because I came very close to losing them and I can't imagine life without either of them. The struggles brought me to a place of empathy, where I deliberately sought for ways to help someone. I needed to be pushed to the brink of suicide, a point that looked like there was no return for me to come to terms with what I was struggling with. I needed to stare death in its eyes to awaken something inside me that showed me that I was fearless and willing to fight this monster... not just for myself, but for so many others.

I needed these struggles. God doesn't create wimpy human beings, but He creates warriors... all of whom have a greater destiny.

ACKNOWLEDGEMENTS

Firstly, I want to thank my precious Father in heaven who refused to give up on me.

I dedicate this book to my precious children, Jordane and Jerry who don't seem to be bothered in the slightest by my brokenness, but continue to love me unconditionally. Thank you darlings, you were my driving force to fight through this. I thank my amazing parents, especially my mother Flora, who stood with me 100% and prayed every waking moment for me to gain my confidence, courage and faith. Your prayers worked ma!

I also dedicate this book to my fantastic best friend Sylvia, who spent countless hours just listening to my tears despite her own. Thank you Hari for your prayers, your love and support and for the Godly guidance I received.

Finally, I dedicate this book to you who are silently suffering with depression or suicidal thoughts due to whatever reason. Your life matters to God and He is longing to help you. If He saved me from taking my life and showed me the value of my life, I can't begin to comprehend what He will do for you. He is real! He loves you and don't forget, your self-worth is not dependent on man, but on who you are before Him.

BIBLIOGRAPHY

Emmons, R. A., & McCullough, M. E. (2003). Counting Blessings Versus Burdens: An Experimental Investigation of. *Journal of Personality and Social Psychology*, 377–389.

Emmons, R. A., & Stern, R. (2013). Gratitude as a Psychotherapeutic Intervention. *Journal of Clinical Psychology*.

Kini, P., Wong, J., McInnis, S., & Ga, N. (2016). The effects of gratitude expression on neural activity. *NeuroImage*.

Toussaint, L., Shields, G. S., Dorn, G., & Slavich, G. M. (2014). Effects of lifetime stress exposure on mental and physical health in young adulthood: How stress degrades and forgiveness protects health. *Journal of Health Psychology*.

Toussaint, L., Shields, G., & Slavich, G. (2016). Forgiveness, Stress, and Health: a 5-Week Dynamic Parallel Process Study. *Annals of Behavioral Medicine*.

Zahn, R., Moll, J., Paiva, M., Garido, G., Krueger, F., Huey, E. D., & Grafman, J. (2009). The Neural Basis of Human Social Values: Evidence from Functional MRI. *Cereb Cortex*, 276-283.

www.ingramcontent.com/pod-product-compliance
Lightning Source LLC
LaVergne TN
LVHW051518070426
835507LV00023B/3172